GOD

IN

ACTION

GOD
IN
ACTION

How Faith in God
Can Address the Challenges
of the World

FRANCIS CARDINAL GEORGE, O.M.I.
ARCHBISHOP OF CHICAGO

DOUBLEDAY RELIGION

NEW YORK LONDON

TORONTO MELBOURNE SYDNEY

DD

DOUBLEDAY

Published in the United States by Doubleday Religion, an imprint of the
Crown Publishing Group, a division of Random House, Inc., New York.
www.crownpublishing.com

DOUBLEDAY and the DD colophon are registered trademarks of
Random House, Inc.

Grateful acknowledgment is made to the following for permission to re-
print previously published material:

The Center for Bioethics & Human Dignity: "Christian Vision for Moral
Decisions in Bioethics" by Cardinal George, an address given at the seventh annual conference of The Center for Bioethics & Human Dignity in
Deerfield, Illinois, on July 21, 2000. Reprinted by permission of the Center
for Bioethics & Human Dignity.

Northwestern University Press: Excerpt from "Letter to Genetically Engineered Superhumans" from *Eulogy for a Private Man* by Fred Dings
(Evanston: Northwestern University Press, 1999). Reprinted by permission
of Northwestern University Press.

Library of Congress Cataloging-in-Publication Data

George, Francis E. (Francis Eugene), 1937–
    God in action : how faith in God can address the challenges
of the world / Francis George.—1st ed.
        Includes bibliographical references and index.
        1. Christian sociology—Catholic Church.   2. Christian sociology—
United States.   3. Catholic Church—Doctrines.   I. Title.
        BX1406.3.G46 2011
        261—dc22

                                                                2010052830

ISBN 978-0-307-59026-8
eISBN 978-0-307-59028-2

PRINTED IN THE UNITED STATES OF AMERICA

Book design by Ellen Ciprano
Jacket design by Laura Duffy
Author photograph: Jeff Ebert

10   9   8   7   6   5   4   3   2   1

First Edition

To the many Catholic priests who,
through prayer and ministry,
live with God and interpret his purposes for his people

Contents

GOD

IN

ACTION

PREFACE

There are many books about religion in public life. This book is not intended to be simply one of them. If the discussion about public life begins with "religion," it usually treats the influence of religious belief on people when they act in their capacity as citizens. Religion then has influence if it shapes the thinking and actions of people who act. It has influence in public life if it shapes the thinking and actions of those who hold public office and those who elect them. If public life is taken to extend beyond the political to other areas where society is created, religion is still usually considered as a set of ideas peculiar to churches or synagogues, mosques or temples, ethical culture groups or moral improvement societies. Religion in this sense is primarily a philosophy of life. It is a public benefit when its practice inspires the altruism necessary for a civil community's common life. It is a public problem when its practice leads to conflict or oppression of various sorts. In all these instances, however, religion is reduced to a set of ideas in competition with other ideologies.

But religion, in the sense in which the term is used in this book, is first of all belief in a God who reveals himself as a God who acts, a God intimately involved in human history. If religion presents only a God who is, at most, a cosmological principle, then it is science that shapes public life. If religion presents only a God who has no existence except as a projection that expresses the sum total of human yearnings, then it is psychology that shapes public life. If religion presents only a God who looks like a nation's citizenry, then politics becomes the highest level of public conversation.

What, however, if God has his own ways that are not always our ways? What if God acts in public affairs in ways that can, of course, be ignored from day to day but at a price for individuals and whole societies? If God is an actor, how is it possible to trace his action? There are books on spirituality, the Exercises of St. Ignatius of Loyola, for example, that help an individual to enter into a unique conversation that leads to a discovery of God's will for him or her. This is not such a book. There are theologies of history that try to discern the grand lines of God's action in shaping the destiny of human societies. This book is not one of them. There are visionary eschatologies that purport to show how human actions fit into God's intentions and then point to how things should be in the end. These pages are nothing so profound.

This book is a modest effort to look for how God acts in the challenges of our times, in this day and age. Can we discover God's actions in the part of human experience that is public in our day? The Second Vatican Council believed we could and challenged Catholics to read the "signs of the times." This injunction was not to be an exercise in self-secularization, as if openness to the times means that the only criteria for making judgments would be provided by this world and on its terms. The Council's challenge was, rather, to detect signs of eternity in the events of our world because the eternal God is at work in our times. The criteria for discerning God's action have to be read from within human events with an eye for discovering a presence that brings good out of evil, hope from despair, and life out of death.

Catholic social theory is based upon reason in conversation with faith. Its basic category is the common good. It presupposes the God revealed by Jesus Christ, who became one of us in order to bring us under God's sovereignty. God's eternal Kingdom is made present now in the Church, the sacrament of God's Kingdom, through which God acts surely and visibly. But God acts through and in all created reality. Just as religion is less a set of ideas than a vehicle for relating to God, the Church is less one more institution within a state than an instrument for relating each of us and the whole world to God.

This book considers the sense in which God is the primary actor in American society because he is the Creator and Savior of the whole world. It then examines a number of issues that challenge our reading of God's influence in public affairs and concludes with a perspective that escapes narrow nationalism by looking for God's action in the movement toward unifying the human family in our day.

A book such as this is the product of many occasions and much advice. I am grateful to those who asked me, on various occasions, to address some of the themes and topics discussed here. I am grateful always to those who helped me create this manuscript, especially to Mr. Thomas Levergood of the Lumen Christi Institute at the University of Chicago, whose urging and reminders and suggestions helped me bring the book to completion. I am grateful as well to Dr. Robert Royal for good advice and good example. His work helped the Doubleday editors. My staff is exemplary in their patience, and many in the Archdiocese of Chicago were understanding of the demands involved in this project, demands that sometimes prevented me from being as available to them as I might have been. I join those who might read this book in thanking all of them.

FRANCIS CARDINAL GEORGE, O.M.I.
Feast of the Immaculate Conception of the Blessed
   Virgin Mary
December 8, 2010

Introduction

God in Action

God's activity has faded from popular consciousness in societies organized publicly as if God did not exist. The history of this development is easy to trace. Its key is the enshrining of autonomy as the preeminent human value and the substitution of progress for providence. God, even in some theological reflection, becomes a force or an inspiration in the deep background of life rather than an agent who shapes human affairs. The fate of religion follows that of God, fading from public consciousness and conversation.

Late medieval philosophies that substituted will for reason weakened the role of intellect in human affairs and placed power at the center of our understanding of what is real, what is being. Without the shared being of all that is, gathered into various natures, only individuals exist and each wills itself into the kind of being it chooses from moment to moment. A being can thus claim to be free only to the extent that it has its way. God, who is all-powerful, does what he wants. God is seen as an individual being whose existence is unrelated to the structures of his creation, which is simply the result of his will. Human freedom, consequently, is rooted in a desire for self-determination. The will is sovereign and chafes when its power is limited. When the infinite will of God inevitably clashes with the finite but unlimited desires of man, something has to give, someone has to go. From this perspective, following the will of God, which is the pattern for holiness of life, does not bring joyful fulfillment to human beings; it leads them to suffer existential contradiction in servitude to an arbitrary divine power.

Modern thinkers have explored this supremacy of will, whether divine or human, to its intrinsic conclusions and have created models of public life compatible with it. In the seventeenth and eighteenth centuries, after the development of individualism in private life during the Renaissance, God's threat to human freedom was minimized by reducing God to a first cause who established the laws of the universe and set the elements of the cosmos in motion. However, in this framework, God plays no essential role in the unfolding of the cosmos or of public affairs in the world. Some deistic thinkers, like Newton, thought God might be occasionally useful to right any cosmic unbalances, but God is, at best, a distant ally of the human project of mastering nature and bending it to human purposes. The universe is a machine wound up by God but historically related to us as a playing field for human activities. This sense of God's activity influenced the development of public life in America through the writings and activities of Thomas Jefferson, Benjamin Franklin, and Thomas Paine.

What God is prevented from doing in this philosophic scenario is truly acting, for action by God would interfere with human freedom. Individuals can freely choose to relate to God in a personal way, but such "religion" is private and can have no normative value for another or for public life. It is a matter of our choice, not God's, how we might relate to a hypothetical "Supreme Being." Eventually, since nature does not disclose who God is in himself, he becomes an unnecessary factor in public intellectual life, and the result is practical atheism; we live together as if God did not exist.

It is true that no one needs the hypothesis of a "God of the gaps," a God who enters like a stagehand, as if there is no qualitative difference between creaturely activity and divine action. Pantheists save some sense of the divine by treating God not as Supreme Being but as the whole of being. Friedrich Schleiermacher (1768–1834), deeply impressed by the critiques of religion proffered in the learned salons of late eighteenth-century Berlin, attempted to formulate a pantheistic version of religion that would be immune to the criticisms of its "cultured despisers." In his hugely influential *On Religion,* Schleiermacher held that religion is "the sense and taste for the infinite,"[1] a mystical feeling for the unlimited ground of being in and through which all finite things exist. In his later works, Schleiermacher describes religion as "the feeling of absolute dependence," that is to say, the relationship that we attribute not to any of the particular things in the world but to being itself.[2] One of the principal marks of Schleiermacher's God is that *he doesn't act.* "Revelation" is any moment when human beings become aware in some fashion of the "whole" of reality. Any breakthrough of the infinite into our consciousness is to be considered a miracle. In the speeches published as *On Religion,* Schleiermacher even compares God to the deep background music of life, something like the tones of a distant organ.

C. S. Lewis's characterization of this kind of mystical pantheism is especially apt. Lewis says that, for many moderns, God is like a book they take off the shelf from time to time in order to feel inspired. But when they are tired of the book, they put it back on the shelf and return to their ordinary preoccupations. Schleiermacher's divine mystical ground is intuited and accessed from *our side,* but it does not itself take any initiative. "God" doesn't act. This form of modern theology has permeated the American consciousness. It entered the American cultural bloodstream through essayists, philosophers, and poets like Ralph Waldo Emerson, Josiah Royce, and Walt Whitman. As with the Deists, the motivation of the mystical pantheists is to clear space for human freedom. As long as God is simply the deep background of life, we can move and choose and act more or less freely; and when God is simply identified with the sum total of all things or with the energy that envelops finite reality, it is a very short step to saying, quite simply, there is no God. Deprived of any nature or of making any valuable contribution, God becomes an empty symbol that can be dangerous to human well-being.

This is the step taken by Ludwig Feuerbach and his army of followers, including Karl Marx and Sigmund Freud. It was Freud who famously dismissed Schleiermacher's "sense and taste for the infinite" as an "oceanic feeling," a remnant of the primitive consciousness that infants have in the womb.[3] When he got around to psychoanalyzing religious people, Freud concluded that they were in the grip of a childish delusion, a wish-fulfilling fantasy that offers false comfort and prevents effective human action.

Feuerbach, Marx, and Freud all gave voice to the typically

modern concern that God, even in a watered-down form, is a threat to full human flourishing. Feuerbach said that we should give up the pathetic I-thou dialogue of prayer and realize we are simply talking to the idealized version of ourselves. Marx said that the sooner we slough off the skin of religion, the sooner we can commence the work for social justice that will transform the world. Freud thought that religion was a neurotic block to integrated consciousness. Sooner or later, those who are sure they are entirely free to determine their own identity and actions without God will deny his existence.

God's dismissal first from modern thinking and then from modern life doesn't mean, of course, that God has really died or is any less absent from human life now than he ever was. But we obviously need to clarify again what we mean by God before we examine how he might be acting in the world. How can we think about God as an actor, an agent in the universe and in human affairs? Essential to this concern is a clear articulation of how God can act without compromising or threatening the integrity of the created realm. How can God's action strengthen rather than threaten human freedom? My own convictions find theoretical support in Thomas Aquinas's understanding of God and the world's relation to him.

For Thomas, the prime referent of the term "being" is God. God is distant from yet intimately related to everything that can be called being, because God gives all things their reality as cause of their very being. To accomplish all this, God can't be *a* being but is, in himself, Subsistent Being, a principle and a person. God is what it means to be, and creatures are those realities that, to varying degrees, reflect and share in the intensity of the divine being because they participate in being according to

their own limited natures. It follows from this conception that
God and creatures should not be categorized side by side, as
though they fall together under the one heading "being." Thomas
specifies that God is not contained in any genus, even the genus
"being." And he therefore draws the logical conclusion that God
cannot be defined and that his being is, properly speaking,
incomparable. Creatures can be said to be like God, but God
should not be said to be like creatures. This is why Aquinas asserts that God is not related to the world; God is closer to us
than we are to ourselves. God does not hover over and against
creatures. Rather, God's creations find their own most profound
identity through their Creator. God not only creates; he sustains
in being the creation he loves.

The Deists got part of this vision of reality right in affirming the otherness of God to the world. God's being is indeed
other than the beings that participate in being. Nevertheless, God's
otherness is not a conventional otherness or separation. God is
the one who, even as he radically transcends the world, remains
the great *Not Another.* The pantheists got part of this vision of
reality right in affirming God's noncontrastive otherness, but
they lost the proper tension by simply collapsing God into the
world. Thomas's delicately balanced metaphysics allowed him to
speak of God as supremely present to the world, necessarily active in it, but not a threat to the integrity of the creatures that he
has made. God can be the ground of freedom and not a competitor to it; he can act in and through every creaturely act, but
without compromising the creaturely integrity of those acts.
Creatures exist because God exists; they act in particular ways
because God has given them a particular nature.

Thomas Aquinas speaks of God's activity in the world in

the first volume of his *Summa theologiae* (Question 22). Thomas analyzes God's goodness and power when he considers how to speak about the creation of the world. He explains that, even though God is eternal and his providence would involve him in the grubby world of time and matter, God nevertheless does act in the world and is responsible for whatever good exists in creatures, since God's providential ordering of things to their proper end is indeed good for creatures. Like an artist creating a picture, God is involved with the way things work in general and in particular, because he created all beings with a proper purpose, a natural end or finality. Helping them achieve that purpose is part of God's action in creating them. God not only initiated the world, he not only sustains it in being, but he actively directs all things—rational and irrational—toward the fulfillment of their proper nature, the directions or longings that are part of their very nature, no matter what that might be.

St. Thomas was aware of the ancients who denied divine governance by asserting that chance rules the universe. He does not answer them by saying that God's governance or providence means the universe is rigidly determined, allowing no room for play or hazard. Rather, he draws on a distinction between universal cause and particular causes in order to address the proper relationship between God's activity and ours. One thing can escape the ordering of a particular cause through the intervention of some other particular cause. For example, I might carefully plan a barbecue only to see it interrupted by the arrival of rain. I planned an event and the weather got in the way. However, nothing can escape the influence of the properly universal cause of being, which necessarily presses upon any and all finite realities. If we limit our gaze to the network of conditioned and interdependent causes, we can indeed speak of chance events. My barbecue got rained out. But if we look at the universe from the viewpoint of eternity or from the standpoint of the cause of the very being of everything, we should speak not of chance but rather of providence. God causes the "being" of a creature's activity or there could be no action at all.

Thomas's image for this is the king who, wanting two of his subjects to meet, sends them on different missions but without informing either of the other's charge. The two men meet, from their perspective, by chance, though their coming together was fully foreseen and arranged by the king. Or we might consider a skilled meteorologist who can explain in great detail why the weather is sunny and warm on a given day. He can articulate the various causes that chanced to make the weather pleasant, and, as far as it goes, his explanation is sufficient. But the meteorologist or any one of us can also invoke the first cause of being, the one who is intelligently responsible for the totality of existence, and can, with confidence and sincerity, thank him for making the day so pleasant.

Both accounts are valid, though the frameworks in which the explanations take place are different. Within the first (the network of conditioned causes), chance, happenstance, and luck are real; within the second (the all-embracing causality of God), they are not. This distinction helps to explain the remark of Pope John Paul II that, for people of faith, there are no coincidences. Again, an example might be the search for a unified field theory in explaining the cosmos, uniting the separate realms of causality that seem to be explained by Newtonian physics on one level and quantum mechanics on another, with the addition of numerous other fields of explanation posited by the discovery of new manifestations of matter and its effects. Looking for God's actions in time by entering the viewpoint of eternity is an analogous intellectual exercise, although what counts for evidence in the two projects is as different as are matter and spirit. God's proper actions are immediate because, as pure spirit, he is not limited by matter or subject to the laws of space and time. But there remain the created limits in which and through which he acts in mediate fashion.

God's good governance of the universe and of our lives is seemingly compromised by the great evils that are part of both nature and history. The world is marked by natural plagues and human wars. The evils that plague human experience have led some moderns to limit God's power, for the less active God is, the more he can avoid blame for the darkness of the world. But a less than infinite and all-powerful God cannot be the Creator of the world, so an answer to the challenge of evil has to be sought again in the differences between orders of causation.

St. Thomas follows St. Augustine in holding that a provider who cares for only a segment of reality excludes evil from his domain as much as he can, while the Provider whose care is the whole of creation permits evils to exist in certain areas of his creation so as to bring out the total good of the whole. In particular, the elimination of all evils would preclude the good of human freedom. For Aquinas, even a free act is ordered to an end; it has a purpose natural to it and, if free, intended by the human actor as agent. If the end is consistent with human nature, then it is done, freely, under the providence of God, whether it is eating a sandwich or researching a cure for cancer. God's influence is not "outside" the structure of our acting; his influence is not an imposition that limits human freedom. His is an activity that makes possible and cooperates with a free human act. God's causality is within the human act itself inasmuch as it is ordered to the good. If the act is disordered, oriented to an evil end, like killing an innocent person, God permits it as a misuse of human freedom, an evil that God in ways unknown to us can still use to his good purpose.

Arbitrary and purely willful self-determination is the antithesis of genuine freedom, an insight that is acknowledged each time an athlete or an artist disciplines immediate desire to make the achievement of some good first possible and then effortless. For many moderns, freedom is fundamentally repugnant to the influence of others; but on Thomas's reading, freedom is naturally ordered to just such influence, precisely because it is ordered to the good. We become free speakers of English not inasmuch as we choose to speak any way we want but rather in the measure that we submit ourselves to a whole series of teachers, to rules of grammar and syntax, and to the examples of great writers and orators. What the will seeks in all its movements is some part of the good, inasmuch as it can be known, and God is quite properly characterized as the good that includes all others. It follows that God is the power that moves the will through attraction in any and all of its acts. Such influence is the very condition of the possibility of freedom, not an imposition in human affairs.

Finally, relating God's infinite power to human freedom in order to account for both explains part of God's providence, his directing of the universe to its proper end. Left to be examined is how God's power works providentially in and through the operations of nature that are not free. One way to preserve God's power, familiar to Aquinas from the thought of philosophers of his time, is to argue that God's operation in nature is so powerful and all-pervasive that natural things do not truly have causal efficacy on their own. While the fire seems to heat the wood, it is really God who is doing the heating. This solution preserves the transcendent power of God by emptying the physical world of its own causal integrity. Instead of removing God so that the world might be free, this solution removes the world so that God can act without interference. Modern ears accustomed to hearing God reduced to "an unnecessary hypothesis" must find this a truly strange notion. More important for Aquinas, it is strange to God himself, who delights in sharing his causal power with creatures. A "Supreme Being" might want to cling to his prerogatives in order to maintain his superiority, but a God who is Being itself has no such difficulty. His goodness is manifest in his capacity to give rise to what is other than himself; his glory is his creatures' participation in his governance.

Aquinas lays out the ways that God acts in and through the operations of nature. First, God gives to all natural agents their very capacity to act as well as their being, since he is always present to the world as its Creator. Second, God, as prime mover, compels all natural agents to act, through either efficient or final causality, through either "push" or "pull." We recognize final causality in animals when we speak of instinct. We ourselves act freely when our own intentions or final purposes are aligned with our proper human nature. Third, God can employ certain created things as his instrumental causes, much as a sculptor uses a chisel or a writer a pen. This kind of divine agency implies that God is "closer" and more present to his effect than is the instrumental cause he uses, just as the artist is more fully engaged with his painting than his brush could ever be. All of this, of course, is but ringing the changes on the great principle of divine noncompetitiveness. Being itself, which is not a being within the world, can, because of God's qualitative otherness to creation, involve finite agents as secondary causes in his own project while, at the same time, they exercise the causality proper to themselves. The battle of mutually exclusive freedoms imagined by modern thinkers is simply foreign to the worldview of Thomas Aquinas.

That worldview, it must be acknowledged, is the creation of human reason informed by religious faith. The book of the prophet Isaiah, upon which Thomas wrote a penetrating commentary, makes eminently clear the universal range of God's creativity. Again and again, the prophet reminds us that God made the whole of finite reality and that no power stands over and against him. He goes so far as to say that God creates both light and darkness, both weal and woe. In some of the most lyrical passages in all of Scripture, Isaiah argues that the true God is, properly speaking, incomparable. He is not one God, however supreme, among many; rather, he alone is God and enjoys a unique status. "To whom then will you liken God? Or what likeness compare with him?" (Is 40:18). "I am the LORD, and besides me there is no savior" (Is 43:11). "Thus says the LORD the King of Israel and his Redeemer, the LORD of hosts: 'I am the first and I am the last; besides me there is no god. Who is like me?'" (Is 44:6–7). "I am the LORD, and there is no other, besides me there is no God" (Is 45:5). "Who told this long ago? Who declared it of old? Was it not I, the LORD? And there is no other god besides me, a righteous God and a Savior; there is none besides me" (Is 45:21). These are not boasts but facts, facts we need to know in order to understand who we are and how we act.

Though the opening lines of the book of Genesis clearly teach that God is the Creator of the "heavens and the earth," which is to say the whole of finitude, there still remains a certain ambiguity in the measure that the primal chaos, the "formless and empty" of the Hebrew text, seems to confront God as a demiurge less than infinite in being and in power. God still seems like a character from cosmogonic myth, drawing order from some preexisting though unformed matter, a shaper but not a creator. But Isaiah goes beyond Genesis and represents a refinement of the Israelite theological consciousness, a deeper perception of the incomparability and universal creativity of the true God. It is this very otherness of the Creator that permits him to enter into the world noninvasively. It is this awareness of who God is in his personal self-revelation to the prophet that informs the way the biblical authors typically describe the dual and noncompetitive agency of God and human beings.

In many Scriptural narratives, God acts through the people and things he created and loves. During a time of great corruption, when the priests and leaders of the people had turned away from God, when Israel was languishing, a simple and childless woman named Hannah begged God for a son. She had no inkling that the child God would give her would emerge as the great prophet Samuel, who would anoint two kings and set the history of salvation on a surer course. But God acted through her desire to be a mother in order to achieve his own purpose in saving the world.

Much later in the story, God has withdrawn his spirit from Saul and has given it to David, but we see this happening through the complex psychological and political maneuverings of the two players. The deteriorating relationship between King

Saul and the once-trusted David can be read as a function of very human jealousy and rivalry for kingship between Saul and his son-in-law, and the war between the houses of Saul and David can be interpreted as an instance of brutal realpolitik. But while natural agents are acting on their own steam and in their own order of created being, God is acting all the while through them for his own purposes, in order to restore to them and all of us the freedom lost in sinning.

In Jesus of Nazareth, divinity and humanity come together so perfectly that a human being, without losing his integrity, can be "the icon of the invisible God." At the Council of Chalcedon (A.D. 451), the Christian Church recognized that Jesus is the personal union of two natures, divine and human, which come together "unconfusedly, indivisibly, immutably, inseparably." This means that nothing of the human in Jesus is undermined and nothing of the divinity in Christ is compromised. In him, two minds (divine and human) as well as two wills (divine and human) meet in utter congruence, so that Jesus' authentically human acts are divine acts, as well, and vice versa. Jesus' properly human freedom is not a block to the divine freedom but an icon of it.

If the God who acts is, in much modern thought, a God dangerous to human freedom and natural activity, then the secularist worldview should be accepted and followed to its consequences, for such a God can be permitted to enter only tentatively and with extreme restriction into the public sphere, if at all. As long as we stand at the foot of the mountain and look up, as Dante did when he was lost in a dark wood, using only our own powers of conceptualization, we will tend to see God as a vague and distant force. Things change dramatically when we take seriously the biblical tradition that presents a God who speaks and acts, who comes down from the holy mountain with a law and with a challenging word that completes in history the word of natural creation and permits conversation and cooperation between himself and his creatures. The irony is that this God, and not the mute, inert God of the philosophers, is, in fact, the friend of human freedom.

How does God act in the challenges of our public lives today? Since the law in American society and culture is often given status as the voice determining our activity and even as the will of God, how the law operates to isolate us from God or to help us cooperate in his designs is extensively considered in Chapters 1 through 3. The first chapter explores the place of God in the complex of American society, which is both secular and religious. Chapter 2 examines the legal context that would limit our recognizing or acknowledging God as a public actor. The sense of human freedom spoken of here is reexamined in Chapter 3 and related to the search for truth in Chapter 4. How our bodies and their sexual activity make us either partners or competitors with God is the subject of Chapter 5. The following chapters examine particular public activities that can strain or even destroy our relationship with God: warfare against enemies, commerce with trading partners, and the reception of foreigners into our society. Chapters 9 and 10 explore how changing global relationships uncover the providential activity of God in this time in human history. These chapters discuss situations in which God is at work; the challenge is to work with him.

I

GOD IN AMERICAN PUBLIC LIFE

Belief in God's presence and action in American public life, in social events, in education, in civic celebrations and political discussions, which for two hundred years had been considered broadly beneficent, changed radically on September 11, 2001. Immediately after the attacks on our country in the name of the God of Abraham, op-ed pieces in some major newspapers made it clear that all doctrinal or dogmatic religion, religion that relies upon a historic revelation by a living God, is a threat to peace. Every religion must therefore give up every claim to truth and base its right to existence only on its offering private consolation and public charity. Religious intellectual claims must be reduced to puny personal spiritual insights that can make no authoritative demands upon anyone else. That religion can be used to excite or justify violence was recognized by Pope John Paul II when he called the leaders of all world religions to Assisi in 1986 and again during the millennium celebrations in order to pray, respectfully, in one another's presence, for peace. Religion, it was hoped, would never be an excuse for violence but must, instead, play the role of peacemaker.

Karol Wojtyla's successor as Bishop of Rome, Joseph Ratzinger, chose the name Benedict because of his expressed desire to be a peacemaker. At his election, in 2005, he recalled St. Benedict and the role of the monasteries in pacifying Europe and preserving classical culture and education after the collapse of the Western Roman Empire in the fifth century. He likewise recalled the memory and purpose of Pope Benedict XV during the First World War. Prevented from arbitrating a cease-fire early in the war and then denied a voice in the creation of the peace treaty, Benedict XV created the Vatican Refugee Service to help reunite families separated by the conflict. Now, Pope Benedict XVI wants to deepen interreligious dialogue in order to make religion instrumental in establishing a peaceful world order.

Religion cannot play the role of peacemaker in any society unless the relation between religion and forms of government is addressed and clarified. Every form of government justifies its own existence through its protection of the people governed and the creation of a public order in which people can be secure and live in peace. In considering the action of God in American society, one must raise the question of the relation between religion and our particular form of government, representative democracy. Democratic government justifies its existence not only because it can keep the peace but also because it can do so while respecting and preserving human freedom. Clarifying the relation between God and public life in American democracy demands attending to preconceived beliefs about the meaning of religion and its manifestations; about modernity and its expressions since the French Revolution; about secularity and its proper but limited realm; and about democracy and its many varieties. Basic to distinctions made here will be the loosely Augustinian distinctions among the sacred, where God is clearly the primary actor; the profane, where God's activity is rejected and excluded; and the secular, the public space where, cooperating with God, the world works out its projects and determines its destiny. After clarifying these three terms, I will argue three propositions that expose some of the difficulties and help us to address some of the reasons for the movement now to secularize our democratic society. In a profanely secularized society, God does act, because he is God; but he does so clandestinely, because he is not allowed to appear in public.

First, a word about religion: almost all historical religions are founded on the belief that God has taken initiative in the affairs of humanity. Religions make truth claims about the nature of God, the nature of the human family, and the destiny of the world and the human race. They and their truth claims are universal, although each major religion is dominant in particular parts of the world. In these places, they have shaped cultures and public life, along with informing the lives of individual believers. Because religion begins with divine initiative, it is not entirely malleable; our experience is not definitive in establishing religious truth. Nor can faith be reduced to personal spirituality. Historical religions have afforded windows to a transcendent order not of our making. They become institutionally visible in churches or religious associations, in monasteries and mosques and synagogues, in organizations of all sorts, especially in the fields of education, health care, and charitable works. In the explicitly religious realm, God or something like a divine presence permeates every dimension of experience, although always through mediators, whether priests or creeds, sacred texts or personal conscience.

Historical religions, because they make truth claims, have been able to create or at least contribute to reasoned public discourse. It is of great importance to distinguish between religion and a personal philosophy of life, a view of things created by a human thinker and actor with no claim to a source transcendent to experience. It is also important, if religion is to be a public voice, that it be able to critically examine its own claims and teachings, using rationally defensible rules for public discourse. Of singular importance in this examination is the question of who God is, for if God is a competitor to human initiative, a type of cosmic dictator, as I discussed in the introduction, then religion will sit uneasily in public conversations in democracies established to protect human freedom.

Religion, as opposed to a personal philosophy, is inevitably communitarian. It depends on texts only to the extent that they have been recognized as sacred by the community in which and for which they were written. God, and therefore religion, demands a total response, a complete personal commitment; but neither God's self-revelation in history nor any religion provides all the practical answers to life in the world. If everything is strictly sacred, then the faith community swallows up the world, and society becomes a monastery. Secularists can then dismiss religion as too sectarian to shape public life. Religion's challenge to a profanely secular worldview, rather, is the recognition of how God acts in areas of human experience that are not explicitly sacred: in law, in warfare, in business, in sexuality, in politics.

Second, a clarification about modernity: modernity, as it has come to characterize the largely Western and now global project of the past three centuries, means the pursuit of this-worldly fulfillment, an enterprise that often puts man at the center of human affairs if not of the universe. It proclaims the autonomy of the human race in pursuing science, the autonomy of the nations in pursuing sovereignty, and the autonomy of individuals in pursuing rights. In order to reduce the impediments or strictures interfering with autonomy, modernity conquers nature itself through scientific understanding and technological change, which is the manipulation of nature for human purposes. Progress in this field has enabled us to control disease on the one hand and to create weapons of mass destruction on the other. Many people, however, still fail to understand both nature and the modern machines that shape nature into our environment. Likewise, in order to reduce the impediments to autonomy that come from other persons or from the state, modernity has developed forms of liberal democracy, protecting rights to worship, think, speak, associate, and own and exchange goods of all sorts. The protection of individual rights, however, has not purged from human memory the idea of the state also as protector of the common good, a staple term in Western political theory throughout the Middle Ages. Modern times have, in fact, been marked by numerous attempts to create a perfect society through social engineering, always justified by one political ideology or another, many careless of or even destructive of human freedoms.

There is, at the heart of the liberal democratic project, a tension recognized by John Locke and James Madison in our own political tradition and by Aristotle and others in classical thought. How can society purposefully and safely use the state to effect the fulfillment of its citizens when power tends to corrupt its holders? The threat of harmful forms of possible state coercion has been contained by constitutions with bills of rights, systems of mixed regimes, separation of powers, and checks and balances. Democracy, considered as the participation of all in politics at least through the election of rulers, is the form of government most consistent with liberalism. But because even democracy carries the risk of majority tyranny, democratic states most concerned with freedom have evolved systems of federalism, of indirect rule through representatives, and of judicial review of legislation.

Alexis de Tocqueville, the French visitor writing about America in 1835, wondered whether democracy's protection of human rights might be lost through its gradual undermining of the sources that gave secure basis to these rights in society: the discipline of virtue and the convictions of religion. Tocqueville linked democracy and secularization because democracy will, over time, he felt, encourage citizens to "deny anything that they cannot understand" and propel people toward "an almost invincible distaste for the supernatural."[1] By contrast, Pope John Paul II, acknowledging the Catholic Church's slow recognition of the positive possibilities in democratic order, came, from his own experience of Nazi and Communist regimes in Poland, to believe that the orderly selection and replacement of rulers by citizens both protect the many from "narrow ruling groups" and enhance human dignity through participation in political choices.

John Paul II, however, echoed elements of Tocqueville's arguments in pointing to the corrosive effect upon democratic ideals by the passage of bad laws. These form people in ways of thought inimical to even constitutionally protected rights. If a democratic society comes to believe, for example, that religious agnosticism and moral relativism are necessary to preserve social peace, truth becomes the enemy of freedom and freedom itself is reduced to individual autonomy. The common life, which participatory democracy was designed to protect, can then be lost to dominant interests divorced from the common good but capable of influencing politics and public life. Democracy is based on more than legal procedures; it needs a shared vision. John Paul II built his defense of liberalism on its positive ability to protect freedoms, including the freedom of the Church to pursue her mission in the world and freedom for all to foster the good of the poor and the working classes through free association and speech and the right to private property with a social mortgage. The Pope was cautiously confident of liberalism's care for the dignity of each person, a normative precept with religious foundation. The democratic state can be confessionally neutral and still be a vehicle for God's activity in the world because people can speak politically in languages open to the transcendent, using value language, for example, without explicitly defining who God is.

Third, a clarification about secularity and secularism: as a total philosophy of public life, secularism captures the world for the profane, the realm from which God is banished. It is not neutral toward claims to truth or rights to act if religion is what sets the terms for the claims or the actions. Public life, from a secularist point of view, must be constructed on the assumption that God does not exist or, if he does, that his existence makes no difference. Secularism's espousal of public atheism in this country is based not on racial superiority, as was the case with Nazi Germany, or on the supposedly scientific history of class warfare, as was the case with Leninist states, but on the myth of human progress carried exclusively by a scientific method limited to the study of material reality. This project occupies the entire ground of public human action and public discourse in the pursuit of truth. In this context, "protection" of individual rights as the uniquely important task of the legal order will eventually destroy not only religious freedom but personal freedom, as well, because both freedoms presuppose that reality is not limited to what is material.

By contrast, an understanding of secularity as the ground between the sacred and the profane displays it as the world of the contingent, with its own penultimate ends and purposes. This understanding does not divorce the world from God, but it recognizes, in Christ's words, that God's Kingdom is not of this world. In a truly free secular society, the institutions that make the sacred visible have a right to act on their own terms and in their own way. Their activity is reflected in the formula of Pope Gelasius I (492–496), reminding Emperor Anastasius as he attempted to control the Church: "There are two powers by which this world is principally governed," not one. While the profane excludes God, the sacred and the secular are both authorized by God, who therefore governs a human race defined by pluralism and institutional diversity. The realm of morality is independent of political decisions but influences them, much as a constitution regulates particular legislation. If religion provides a legitimate ground for officially secular concern with penultimate things, then the secular must provide legitimate ground for religion to address ultimate things on their own terms.

Freedom of religion extends beyond freedom of personal

conscience and beyond freedom to worship. It includes freedom for religious institutions to have a public voice, to be public actors. To illustrate this point, compare freedom of the press to freedom of religion. If newspaper publishers and editors were free to believe what they liked and to organize their companies and employees according to good business practices but were forbidden to speak to issues of public policy, unable to criticize public officials or institutions, restricted to printing for general consumption only what the law or dominant public opinion permitted, there would be no freedom of the press. Yet this is exactly the straitjacket in which religion is placed today by secularists who espouse a seemingly democratic public morality and insist that any public religious critique is illegitimate. Religious institutions are by their properly communal nature public actors. When secular life is constituted without respect for religious freedom, it becomes profane, and persecution of religion becomes inevitable. There is no guarantee that even democratic institutions will prevent this outcome. Independent courts, a free press, an elected legislature can all be manipulated, and have been in our own history, to subvert various freedoms and reflect the prejudices of controlling interest groups as well as those of ordinary citizens. In the public realm, in activities that fill the world from one time to the next, free religious institutions are the primary but not exclusive vehicles for God's actions. His purposes in the world can be fulfilled even by those who deny him; prophets often understand this, which is why they are prophets and why a healthy civil government does not prejudice their activity.

Does this mean that a sane understanding of the sphere of secularity demands there be no restrictions on religious institutions? Of course not, and I will examine some shortly. But the nature of a well-ordered world open to the sacred places restrictions on governments, as well, even on democratic governments. Restrictions on democratic polity should extend not only to governmental institutions but also to the range of human concerns these can legitimately address. A government that determines what is a religious ministry and what is not, what is the nature of an institution such as marriage, which predates both Church and state and is the creature of neither, when human life begins and when it can be taken without a penal trial has exceeded the boundaries of limited governance and is already on the road to totalitarianism. While democratic in form, it has betrayed human freedom.

A final word to define the secular: the world is the place where two key conversations take place, the conversation between faith and culture and that between faith and reason. The dialogue between faith and culture is necessary because both are normative systems; both tell us what to do, what is important, what should be our hierarchy of values. If the norms of faith and the norms of culture are totally antithetical, the believer lives a schizophrenic life and cannot act in good conscience and without constraint. The dialogue between faith and reason is also necessary because both faith and reason search for and espouse truth. If what one professes as a believer and what one thinks as a philosopher or scientist or ordinary citizen cannot be reconciled, skepticism becomes the intellectual order and doubt paralyzes the possibility of common action. A society where faith cannot be a public dialogue partner is by definition totalitarian or at least nonpluralist; such a secularist culture is cut off from dialogue with most of the human race, with consequent misunderstanding tragically inevitable. For the sake of public argument, faith should be permitted to enter into conversation using inspired language from the written witnesses to God's self-revelation in history, but it is also aided by argument that, using reason, does not appeal immediately to particular beliefs. For Catholics, such a language is available, at least in principle, in natural law theory, which defines moral norms by looking at the nature of human actions and their natural finality.

Last, a further clarification about democracy, that political arrangement most protective of human freedom: a theory of democratic governance assumes, against many modern social theorists, that government is more than a form of legal coercion. It brings together individual freedom and the common good, space for individual initiative and united action for common purposes. It exercises a form of authority in which sovereignty is never completely transmitted and where equality before the law does not destroy natural communities, such as marriage and the family, religious associations, business enterprises, and voluntary groupings of all kinds with their proper leaders and officers. Its own political institutions presuppose, sustain, and encourage those associations that create a morality of responsibility for the whole, especially religious institutions that train people in the virtues necessary for self-sacrifice. Democracy depends on a vision of what it means to be human *that it itself cannot provide.*

I would like to propose three arguments that build on these definitions of the secular, of the profane, and of the sacred. Everyone in American public life believes in and defends democratic government. It's not that we believe the world has arrived at an end of history in which everything else has been tried, has failed, and democracy is the only form of government left standing. There are abroad in the world some very potent challengers to the American sense of democracy. Yet those who appreciate what modern democracy has meant in the past must also be among those most concerned about what may be happening to it in the present and future. Our recognition that democracy has no serious rival at the moment as a philosophy and as a basically good form of human government does not prevent us from reflecting critically on it, both in theory and in practice. In this, we follow an American tradition, beginning with the Declaration of Independence, of seeking a more perfect union, present perfection evidently being regarded by our Founders as less than we should hope for.

SECULARISM AS DANGER TO FREEDOM

My first argument, therefore, is that, in the United States, the primary danger to democratic freedoms comes not from religion but from philosophical secularism. Even before embarking on this line of reasoning, however, I believe we must acknowledge that religions themselves have been agents in secularizing public life in America. Jews were often leaders in secularizing our society because they felt doing so was the best way to guarantee that one did not have to be Christian to be American. Analogously, Catholics contributed to secularization in various ways to be sure one did not have to be Protestant to be American. Because all of us have been basically united in our regard for democracy in America, we have until quite recently cultivated a moderate pluralism in public life. Now, however, it seems a battle has arisen between our older notion of a civic pluralism accommodating the religious beliefs of the vast majority of Americans on the one hand and, on the other hand, an aggressive secularism that seems quite intent on eliminating any religiously motivated idea, speech, or action in civic and intellectual life. In the former Soviet Union, the League of the Militant Godless fought from 1935 to 1947 against religion among workers. American analogues seem now to be a growing part of the public scene.

Some have recently argued that pluralism by its very nature demands civic secularism. There seems to be no logical reason why respect for the beliefs of more than a quarter billion Americans, 90 percent of whom declare themselves to be religious, should require us now to eschew the public expression of religion, even in discussing political affairs that have moral foundations or implications. It is, of course, true that politics is not a sacral activity and should not be the carrier of ultimate meaning. Very often, however, political issues do not even yield to rational analysis, with or without a substratum of religious concern. We can easily think of any number of political or economic questions—state versus federal jurisdiction, the minimum wage, treaty agreements—that remain obscure after extensive analyses that are properly secular, even if they have some general religious or moral dimension. We believe, for example, that all human beings are made in the image of God, but that does not give us an automatic answer about the nation's health care system. And we may think that God has made us free and rational without being sure about how much the law may legitimately curtail freedom for the sake of public order. Our religious traditions must recognize certain issues as beyond their proper expertise.

At the same time, the properly secular society has to be sober in its recognition that it exists under God, firm in its understanding that fundamental truths, many of them religious in nature, undergird its very existence, and prudent in determining the good that can and cannot be achieved under given circumstances. This recognition and this determination on the part of secular society are explored in the topics that are the subject matter of this book. The chapters that follow argue that the greatest danger to freedom today arises when the public order that Christians, Jews, Muslims, agnostics, atheists, and others inhabit together is administered by a strict secularism. Religious people cannot agree about their beliefs or doubts, it is often said, so they must leave them aside in deliberations about how they are to live in public together. This seeming neutrality is not at all neutral. Secularism's contemporary claim to be the unique public philosophy of America was probably the central factor in the rise of what is sometimes referred to as the Religious Right, in reaction not to neutrality but to a perceived antireligious bias heading in the general direction of seeking to eliminate religion from public discourse. Such elimination is very unlikely in America; even seventy years of official atheism backed by the gulag did not eliminate all belief in the former Soviet Union. As the contemporary Polish philosopher Leszek Kolakowski has said: "Religious need cannot be excommunicated from culture by rationalist incantation. Man does not live by reason alone."[2]

Far from espousing noncontroversial neutrality, aggressive secularism itself has fostered some of our most heated debates by pushing issues like gay marriage and abortion in a society that would not have come to them by democratic choice. Some would trace divisiveness in public life exclusively to religious views. But secularism has been as divisive as—and perhaps more so than—any other current viewpoint. In sum, as befits a movement that espouses as many controversial views as any other ideology, secularism today cannot be thought of as a healing, neutral, reconciling space in a divided culture. It is one more ideology without rational foundation in the common good.

Cardinal Ratzinger, now Pope Benedict XVI, once said we can see that human reason in a fallen world has a tendency to go dangerously awry, and it is because of this fact that one of the benefits of the dialogue of faith and reason is "the convalescence of reason."[3] In questions about the nature of human sexuality and the protection of human life, for example, we all sense a bewildering shift in the way reason has been divorced from the demands of the common good and we see the imposition of sharp limitations on the kinds of reasoning that are admissible in public debate. Narrow views are presented as humane and rational; broader ones are judged "sectarian." A larger and more adequate historical vision fosters, instead, a deep sense of the importance of believers for the protection of the properly secular. A skeptical secularism fails to provide a foundation for human rights and undermines the foundation that historically has existed to protect them. Secular republics need inspiration about the nature of the person and of liberty that they cannot find within themselves. Secular societies depend on religious and moral traditions to provide this depth. Most ordinary citizens in a country like the United States understand this intuitively, even if they do not always articulate it.

John Paul II, the great pope of the modern struggle with totalitarianism, warned in his 1993 encyclical *Veritatis splendor,* on the relation between truth and the moral life:

Today, when many countries have seen the fall of ideologies which bound politics to a totalitarian conception of

the world—Marxism being the foremost of these—there
is no less grave a danger that the fundamental rights of
the human person will be denied and that the religious
yearnings which arise in the heart of every human being
will be absorbed once again into politics. This is *the risk of
an alliance between democracy and ethical relativism,* which
would remove any sure moral reference point from political and social life, and on a deeper level make the ac-
knowledgement of truth impossible. Indeed, if there is no
ultimate truth to guide and direct political activity, then
ideas and convictions can easily be manipulated for reasons of power. As history demonstrates, a democracy without values easily turns into open or thinly disguised
totalitarianism.

In a democracy, the full range of human values must be
admitted for consideration. Pluralism must mean that all individuals and groups are welcome to participate in the public
debate, whether they are religious or not. What best protects the
foundation of this legitimate pluralism? Three candidates are
evident today: religion itself, purely secular philosophy, and scientific theory.

The Founders of the American constitutional experiment
in well-ordered democratic government thought that religion
played a crucial role in protecting legitimate pluralism. George
Washington's Farewell Address explains that "of all the disposi-
tions and habits which lead to political prosperity, religion and
morality are indispensable supports. . . . And let us with caution indulge the supposition that morality can be maintained
without religion. Whatever may be conceded to the influence

of refined education on minds of peculiar structure, reason and experience both forbid us to expect that national morality can prevail in exclusion of religious principle."[4] Washington evidently distrusted mere speculation in politics, believing that religion is a spring of "popular virtue" and that without "national morality" a free system could not survive. Washington was arguing against Jefferson, who certainly advocated the constitutional separation of Church and state. But Jefferson also wrote in his *Notes on the State of Virginia:* "Can the liberties of a nation be thought secure when we have removed their only firm basis, a conviction in the minds of the people that these liberties are the gift of God? That they are not violated but with his wrath?"[5]

At the very least, the historically religious insistence on both the freedom and the responsibility of the human person helps us to understand what a properly secular and pluralist society should protect. I would go even further and say that human life and public order cannot flourish without the strong presence of some religious features. In that sense, a modern state should not and cannot be neutral between belief and nonbelief. The purpose of religion, of course, is not first of all to protect democracy or any other civil order, but faith does supply ultimate perspectives and fosters human virtues that a merely secular order cannot generate from within itself. To say this is to advocate neither theocracy nor the removal of atheists from public life. It is to stand in the original and realistic American vision of democratic society.

There have also been powerful and well-intentioned efforts to address civil foundations by grounding our respect for one another and our practice of liberty only in purely procedural arrangements. The most prominent of these arguments is found

in John Rawls's *Theory of Justice.* In that seminal work about a
way to create a just society, foundations are simply banished and
we are all seen as acting from behind "a veil of ignorance" in
deciding what public rules we want to adhere to, knowing that
they may be applied to us and to our loved ones. Rawls himself
realized his book presumed that people behind the veil would
be acting according to ideologically liberal principles, which is to
say that they would follow mostly progressive social assumptions
and would elevate things like tolerance for diverse lifestyles over
more substantive commitments. In 1993 he published *Political
Liberalism,* which acknowledged the problems with his earlier
formulation, not least that Americans are not philosophically
liberal and have become markedly less so in the last quarter of
the twentieth century. *Political Liberalism* tried to encourage
Americans to see that, in a pluralistic society, all have an interest
in not making comprehensive, ultimate commitments the norms
for political life. Instead, what Rawls calls "public reason" must
guide public deliberations, but it is a reason without foundation
in anything other than our own processes. At the end of the
day, Rawls and many a lesser theorist appear to be searching
for ways for the secular order to maintain newly discovered
rights to abortion and homosexual activity without seeming to
contradict their own openness to all forms of rationality; they
fall back into asserting a comprehensive liberalism under the
guise of neutrality.

The strictly secular pluralist who seeks to exclude religion
from public life bumps up against the fact that, once you really
allow the voices of various people to be heard, they will be over-
whelmingly religious because the human race is overwhelm-
ingly religious. Not only would Abraham, Moses, David, Judas

Maccabaeus, Jesus, Peter, Paul, Augustine, Aquinas, Maimonides, Dante, Luther, Erasmus, Calvin, Thomas More, Ignatius of Loyola, Pascal, Coleridge, Chateaubriand, Mauriac, Pasteur, Schweitzer, Graham Greene, Einstein, Martin Luther King, Jr., and many other great intellectual figures in the Judeo-Christian tradition be excluded from the public conversation, but so would Thales, Heraclitus, Plato, Aristotle, Virgil, Mohammed, and a host of nonbiblical and non-Western figures, as well. Any intellectual tradition that did not allow such voices into the discussion would be narrow, and any political regime that excluded them could hardly be called pluralist or democratic. It would be a profane secularism seeking to swallow up everything or ignore everyone outside its own narrow purview.

Today, a foundation for a sane secular order is sometimes sought only in materialistic theories that appeal to science for support. The British neo-Darwinian biologist Richard Dawkins has publicly admitted: "I believe, but I cannot prove, that all life, all intelligence, all creativity and all 'design' anywhere in the universe, is the direct or indirect product of Darwinian natural selection."[6] This profession of faith makes admirably clear that scientific rationalism is not as watertight as some people once thought and puts Dawkins and others like him among believers, albeit of a peculiar kind. Such sectarians think they should be able to impose their views on us all through schools and other state instruments. He has asserted that raising children in a religious household is a form of child abuse, that Moses was like Hitler, and that the New Testament espouses sadomasochism.

Yet Dawkins is not wholly ready to accept even his own arguments. He seems quite pointlessly enraged at religious people who, in his system, are only the necessary products of blind natural forces. But why do human beings show a near-universal disposition to believe something that neo-Darwinism claims is unreal? Why does a false picture of the world aid our chances of survival? Some scientists have simply asserted that there must be an adaptive, evolutionary value in belief, which is "hardwired" into our brains and may even stem from a "God gene." Perhaps so, but like the genes that enable us to do science and mathematics, the God gene alone cannot tell us whether its products are true, a question that, amid the countless entities in a vast cosmos, is asked only by human beings. Maybe Dawkins's anger and our failure to conform to strict scientific categories are both symptoms of something that needs attention from a more neutral science. Especially in the face of death, whether that of a person or of entire cultures and countries, questions arise that open the human spirit to propositions beyond the empirical, questions that ask again whether the human saga is all "sound and fury, signifying nothing." To refuse to look at these questions or discuss them truncates human existence and betrays human intelligence.

Although secularism is not logically entailed by pluralism, might there be something in human nature that inexorably leads individuals and masses in conditions of modern freedom to embrace secularism and radical individualism? For an answer, it might be better to look to history and the social sciences rather than to physics and biology. We can at least observe that pluralism in modern conditions seems to exert a gravitational force on a significant sector of the population, especially those in highly sensitive institutions, like the media, the universities, and other shapers of contemporary public culture, to espouse the view that "scientific" secularism is the only legitimate foundation of democracy in our circumstances. But cultures, like individuals, change over time. At the end of the day, at least for the believer, human beings are free and open to graces and energies that, as history repeatedly shows, were not and cannot be anticipated. The prospects for religion in postmodern societies may seem unfavorable. Still, there is no reason why the religious impulses that seem, even to the neuroscientists, to be hardwired into us may not find new ways of public expression. For pluralism and secularism to prevent that development, they would have to produce something like a change in human nature, a new man. Scientific socialism was not up to the task with quite powerful methods at its disposal, and I do not believe scientific secularism will be, either.

DEMOCRATIC INSTITUTIONS
AS DANGER TO FREEDOM

My second argument is that secularism and its attendant danger to freedoms protected by democratic political institutions can arise from those very institutions themselves. I would like to take as a case in point the jurisprudence of the U.S. Supreme Court on religious liberty since the days of Justice Felix Frankfurter, who was on the Court from 1939 to 1962. The history of law in this country exposes our cultural history, for law is the most important unifying factor in a country as diverse as ours. Law exercises a pedagogical function along with its coercive power. It is primarily from the law that we learn how to live as Americans. Recognition in our earlier history that divine law was a guide and corrective to positive law kept open a legal vehicle for God's activity in public affairs. Nature and nature's God could be appealed to; our Creator endowed us with natural rights. That opening has now been legally closed.

What does constitutional law now teach us about religious freedom in our country? To put it simply, it seems to me that the Court has not yet denied that religious freedom is a human right, a more than civil right, but it has tended to regard the public expression of religion as divisive and something the social order has to regard with some suspicion. For example, in the case of *Lemon v. Kurtzman* (1971), the Court declared that state financial aid that directly includes parochial schools violates the establishment clause because the potential for "political fragmentation and divisiveness" along religious lines "is a threat to the normal political process" and is "one of the principal evils against which the First Amendment was intended to protect" society. That our society is so fragile that it needs such protection would be surprising to the citizens of other countries. Great Britain and Australia, New Zealand and most of the Canadian provinces, France, Italy, and most of the European democracies, the State of Israel, and even Iraq under the Baathist regime of Saddam Hussein have given financial aid to the parents of Catholic schoolchildren. With the exception of Saddam Hussein's Iraq, all were and are functioning democracies whose internal unity is not weakened by families seeking a fair pluralism in order to educate youngsters in ways their parents desire.

Does the existence of such families itself contribute to divisiveness? The obvious danger here is that, if every difference is evidence of divisiveness or even discrimination, then eliminating divisiveness and discrimination will justify eliminating all differences, including religious differences, cultural differences, gender differences, racial differences, everything, perhaps, except economic differences in a commercial republic, whose business is business, as Calvin Coolidge once remarked. The Court now seems to understand religious liberty as a means to avoid irrational coercion and civil conflicts rather than as a means to advance an important foundation of human dignity and a legal recognition that God is an actor in human affairs.

The Court has rightly refused to be drawn into questions of religious truth claims, but its reluctance to distinguish between historical religion and any personal philosophy of life demonstrates only a concern to protect the rights of autonomous individuals. This caution clashes with a more traditional understanding of a religious believer as someone owing duties and loyalties to two distinct but sovereign powers. A doctrine resting on the premise that anything counts as religion will also find it very difficult to afford strong protection to the free exercise of religion, for fear that every individual will eventually be a law unto himself or herself. The consequence of this incoherence is twofold: freedom of religion is deinstitutionalized and assimilated to the right of each person to self-expression, even if that expression happens to be religious; and such a thin rights claim puts religion in the position of every other competing societal claim, despite freedom of religion's being the first of our constitutionally guaranteed liberties. Religious institutions are left without the legal protections originally accorded in the First Amendment of the Constitution.

Government institutions, under the pressure of incoherent and unpredictable case law, have predictably engaged in self-censorship. Sacred music in concerts, a drawing of a saint, Valentine's Day cards have all been banned from public schools in recent times. What is taught in such prohibitions is not state neutrality but state disdain for religion. Disdain seems quite evident, to me at least, in the 1990 decision to allow the state to impose even a substantial burden on a believer's religious observance so long as the legal coercion on religious beliefs is a general law without discriminatory purpose and the obligation it imposes makes policy for everyone and every institution. This interpretation of the First Amendment, when applied to Catholic health care and social services, will mean the withdrawal of the Church from many public ministries. It is historically ironic that we are reducing freedom of religion in the United States to freedom of private conscience and worship, the same sense of religious freedom found in the constitution of the former Soviet Union.

I have chosen egregious examples, for the Court has also protected religious freedoms; but the trends point, I believe, to a First Amendment doctrine that permits government to limit the ability of religious believers to live out their commitments fully in public life. This interpretation opens up further threats that the state may burden and discriminate against religious practices and even eliminate the existence of religiously governed organizations if they are engaged in public activities. All this will be done in the name of civil rights for individuals, the only rubric governing public policy in a "liberal" secularist state.

The fact, moreover, that the First Amendment is now interpreted to permit such developments does not necessarily mean that governments will choose to use their constitutional powers to further dilute religious liberty and secularize society. We still have a largely religious population in many parts of our nation; but to the extent that religious believers should become a minority, they will have few constitutional protections to fall back on. Democratic institutions, like the Supreme Court, can and have become agents of an oppressive secularization.

THE DEMOCRATIC STATE
AS DANGER TO FREEDOM

My third argument about secularization and democracy arises with particular force in the United States. It can happen that democracy does not control or eradicate religion but simply replaces it. American civil religion is the case in point here. The line between a religious duty of patriotism and the replacing of religion by the state is thin and negotiated with difficulty. But as historical religion can be and has been co-opted by a state for its own purposes, so also can it be replaced by devotion to the nation itself when national purpose takes on the character of a religious mission. National symbols can easily pass from demanding our respect and even affection to commanding our ultimate loyalties; but a nation can never be a church, much less an object of quasi-religious worship.

It could be argued that the man who, in saving the union as a sacred duty, did much to found American civil religion is also the one who gave us civil religion's antidote. In his Second Inaugural Address, inscribed on the walls of the Lincoln Memorial in Washington, D.C., Abraham Lincoln wrestled with the intentions of a God of history. Lincoln's God was not a deistic principle, limited to giving us rights and duties, the God of nature, the God of some of the Founders. Lincoln's God, at least by the end of the Civil War, was clearly a provident God, and our duty, as Americans, was to read his intentions in human history without co-opting him to our national purposes.

After reviewing the tragedy of the blood that had been shed on both sides in the fraternal slaughter that was the Civil War, Lincoln declared: "The prayers of both could not be answered; that of neither has been answered fully. The Almighty has His own purposes. . . . Fondly do we hope, fervently do we pray, that this mighty scourge of war may speedily pass away. Yet, if God wills that it continue, until all the wealth piled by the bondsman's two hundred and fifty years of unrequited toil shall be sunk, and until every drop of blood drawn with the lash, shall be paid by another drawn with the sword, as was said three thousand years ago, so still it must be said 'the judgments of the Lord are true and righteous altogether.'"

On another occasion, Lincoln called Americans "an almost chosen people," but there is no room in his final understanding of American loyalties for self-righteousness or for self-vaunting. Even as he wrestled with the horrors of war, Lincoln trusted that God had his own vision for the world, often not understood and sometimes antithetical to our own. The mystery of evil remains unresolved, and this very conundrum warns us against secular utopian schemes. This is perhaps the ultimate protection against a purely civil religion as a form of secularization: that God cannot be co-opted and remains always the primary actor in our history and our endeavors. Since God's will is complex, so must be our affairs. In the long run, any attempt to reduce the complexity of the relations among the sacred, the properly secular, and the profane is doomed to failure, although each such effort can cause great human hardship in the short run. But in both the short and the long run, the Church, or the synagogue, or the mosque or the temple, is where you go when you want to be connected to the One who relates to everyone and every people. If the Church is where one goes to be truly free, how does the Church contribute to our understanding of who we are and what we should do in the activities that shape the world we live in, that fill the theater of secularity?

The answer depends, in part, on how free the Church is to act and how protected she is by the constitution that controls public discourse and life in the United States.

RELIGIOUS LIBERTY IN THE U.S. CONSTITUTION: GOD IN THE DOCK

God's "freedom" to act and freedom for his followers to act in the public order in his name evolve in a broad cultural context shaped by law and other societal influences, but one can also analyze the situation more narrowly, as a purely legal matter. It will help to take the understanding of religious liberty in *Dignitatis humanae* (1965), the document on religious liberty from the Second Vatican Council, and compare it with some of the jurisprudence of the U.S. Supreme Court over the intervening years. How does the U.S. legal understanding of religious liberty make room for God's activity as understood by a council of the Church? If these two ways of understanding religious liberty are greatly different, citizens who are believers will experience tension in their public life.

As a purely legal matter, of course, religious liberty in the United States is simply whatever the Supreme Court says that it is at any given time. In this sense, the future of religious liberty is absolutely guaranteed, since it would be legally impossible to violate a right to religious liberty that the Supreme Court does not recognize as legal. If the Supreme Court says the First Amendment secures only a right to believe whatever one wishes privately, then curtailment of other aspects of religious liberty and religious life will not be a legal restriction on religious liberty, no matter how unjust a believer might think such restrictions to be. In other words, in order to have a substantive conversation about religious liberty in law, we need to distinguish its components. Does it mean liberty of conscience in the individual sense? Does it mean liberty of worship? Does it mean the freedom to evangelize, to teach children, to influence the public order? Religious liberty can legally mean all of this or very little of it, depending on what the Supreme Court decides.

It's not exactly clear at any given time what our Supreme Court is saying about religious liberty, because the jurisprudence isn't totally consistent. Yet before making an assessment, we need to come to an understanding of what is meant by the term itself. What are the components that would seem essential to religious liberty? *Dignitatis humanae* gives five touchstones for measuring commitment to an authentic doctrine of religious liberty from the viewpoint of a Catholic community concerned with following God's will in public life. Those norms are (1) religious liberty is rooted in a proper understanding of human dignity as given by God; (2) religious liberty is necessary so that persons may fulfill their duty to seek the truth, to embrace it, and to live in conformity with the truth, once it has been discovered and accepted; (3) since religion constitutes an essential good of persons who are intelligent and able to seek the truth, it is also an aspect of the common good. The state thus has a duty to foster and aid the religious life of the people, without unfairly burdening irreligious persons or groups; (4) the essential characteristic of religious liberty as a civil matter is noncoercion in regard to religious belief and practice, with the limit always being the just demands of public order; and (5) churches and religious organizations of all sorts must be free, first of all, to govern themselves and, second, to pursue their goals in education, formation of believers, charitable pursuits, and advancement of a more just social order. Those are the essential components of religious liberty in *Dignitatis humanae,* and they undergird the conversation between the right to freedom of religion and current U.S. Supreme Court jurisdiction.

First, as the title of the ecclesiastical document suggests, the bishops of the Second Vatican Council stressed that religious liberty is grounded in a proper understanding of human dignity and, ultimately, in the will of God for his creatures. Human beings need religious liberty because they are created in the image and likeness of God, with rational souls and with free will. God has implanted in human beings a natural desire to seek and to know transcendent truths, not just empirical truths. Thus, the right to religious liberty exists prior to, and regardless of, its recognition by any civil authority. It is not reducible to a civil right. It is a human right, a natural right.

The Supreme Court has not, of course, made a definitive pronouncement on the question of where religious liberty rights are grounded. It would appear that the Court is precluded, in fact, by the Constitution's forbidding the establishment of religion from explicitly agreeing with the position of the Second Vatican Council, since government can't endorse particular religious teaching. On occasion, however, the Court will explain its understanding of the *purpose* of the First Amendment. It often does this, as mentioned in the preceding chapter, in terms of the need to avoid divisiveness and civil discord, a concern not explicit in *Dignitatis humanae.*

In *Lemon v. Kurtzman* (1971),[1] referred to in the last chapter, the Court declared that state financial aid that includes parochial schools violates the establishment clause because the potential for "political fragmentation and divisiveness" along religious lines "is a threat to the normal political process" and is "one of the principal evils against which the First Amendment was intended to protect" society. In a more recent case, *Lee v. Weisman* (1992), the justices explained that the practice of inviting a member of the clergy to offer a nondenominational prayer at a school graduation ceremony was inherently divisive, was coercive toward children, and amounted to a state embrace of the view that "human achievements cannot be understood apart from their spiritual essence."[2] In other words, the public school coerced the children into sitting passively during the prayer, robbed them of a meaningful experience, and undermined the importance of their achievements by "forcing" them to listen to a benediction. These conclusions were well intended, despite the fact that there was little or no evidence of any divisiveness. The Court simply asserted the possibly negative effects of public prayers without considering the possibility that communities might, in fact, be brought together by such practices. Lost in the concern about religious divisiveness is the recognition that religious belief protects human dignity.

Second, in the understanding of the Second Vatican Council, the ultimate *end* or *goal* of religious liberty is that all human beings have the opportunity to come to know and live in the fullness of truth. Human persons can pursue this goal only when they are respected as free and responsible subjects. *Dignitatis humanae* (1965) puts it this way: "The truth cannot impose itself except by virtue of its own truth, as it makes its entrance into the mind at once quietly and with power."[3]

A society should respect religious liberty because this transcendent goal, truth seeking, is one aspect, perhaps the most important aspect, of the good of the person and therefore of the common good of society. People need freedom in order to pursue their highest ends, in order to seek and to embrace the truth. Those whose lives are shaped by adherence to the truth will contribute to a just and stable society. The nature of human freedom and the nature of truth preclude an outside force from simply imposing what is true. Instead, religious liberty contributes to a spirit of openness to the search for truth, especially through education and respectful exchanges. The views of all must be respected, even if judged objectively erroneous, because to do otherwise would make it all the more difficult for those holding them to one day find and embrace objective truth. Many in the United States are somewhat ill at ease in talking about freedom and truth in the same breath because a claim to objective truth can be seen as a threat to personal freedom. But this difficulty should itself be addressed publicly.

The late Pope John Paul II pointed out that the cultural fault line that led to the internal contradiction of the communist system pitted social justice against personal freedom. In denying one for the sake of the other, the whole system was brought down. Toward the end of his life, John Paul II pointed out that an analogous fault line runs through Western culture. Insisting upon objective truth, especially in religious matters, is now regarded as a threat to subjective personal freedom rather than as a condition for freedom's fulfillment. But if there is no way to resolve questions of truth and freedom in matters essential to a well-ordered society, public order is based on force and becomes inherently unstable.

There are two aspects of U.S. religious liberty doctrine in tension with this second norm from *Dignitatis humanae*. First, the Supreme Court correctly says that it has no role in determining the truth claims of various religions. This stance is proper so far as it goes, since governments lack the competence to judge transcendent religious matters. But the Court has taken this sensible restraint to an extreme point that makes it all but impossible to define what counts as "religion." Several decisions have suggested that any and all kinds of personal belief, no matter whether they are totally irrational or wildly idiosyncratic, are "religion," even when those who hold the views themselves explicitly disavow properly religious belief. Some Court cases have even included secular humanism under the rubric of religion. The inability to determine what is a religion and, equally, to distinguish it from a philosophy of life contributes to the incoherence of the Court's doctrine, particularly with respect to free exercise. The Court might recapture some coherence by returning to an understanding of the original meaning of "religion" as used by the Founders. According to at least one scholar, "religion" at the time of the writing of the U.S. Constitution meant a theistic belief system, with a God to whom one owed a set of duties and from whom one could expect reward or punishment in the next life.[4] Such a definition, which recognizes that religious liberty goes beyond the merely ethical, would at least be a starting point for building a coherent approach to the First Amendment, a base on which to ground free exercise and nonestablishment protections.

Furthermore, the Court seems to have assumed that the end or goal of the First Amendment is *not* that everyone should be assisted in accepting the fullness of truth, religious or otherwise, free from discrimination or favor toward one religion and against another, but rather that we must create a secular public culture marked by indifference to religion. The establishment clause has been interpreted to require that only laws with a "secular purpose," primarily secular effects, and no entanglements with religion will be constitutional. The Court argues that the *Lemon* test is necessary not only to prevent religious influence over the state but also to prevent religion from being "taint[ed] with a corrosive secularism."[5] This concern to protect religion rests on unproven assertions that there be no public connection between government and religion in any sense and asserts without evidence that any government involvement with religion is necessarily corrosive or secularizing of religion itself. But numerous examples of cooperation between religion and churches based on mutual respect have demonstrated the contrary. Long before President George W. Bush and his administration moved to recognize faith-based initiatives, there were many cases where the government and the churches (and synagogues) had cooperated without any detriment to the authenticity of religion and with great benefit to society. Catholic Charities' sponsoring low-cost housing or various diocesan programs to feed the poor would be cases in point, along with the institutional services of Catholic hospitals and colleges that depend upon government support.

Another instance of this kind of jurisprudence is the 1948 Supreme Court case *McCollum v. Board of Education,*[6] which reviewed the practice worked out between a school district and a coalition of religious groups. A more benign accommodation between religion and state institutions could hardly be imagined. Parents could agree to allow their children to be released from class to attend a half-hour religious educational program once a week run within the public school building by their church, synagogue, or other religious organization. Children whose parents did not wish them to attend could go to study hall instead. This program was found to violate the establishment clause because it allegedly undermined the secular character of the school day, where the government's goal was to erase religious distinctions. Among other problems, it made children aware of their religious differences and "actively furthered the inculcation of religious tenets" in secular government buildings.[7] The Court held that religious education was to be provided only in the home or the church, never in any public place that might imply governmental approval of a religion.

The Court has been even more explicit about this secularizing goal in recent years, forbidding government actions that might give the impression to a "reasonable observer" that the government was "endorsing" "religion in general" over "irreligion." Putting aside the fact that no one knows what "religion in general" is or what "irreligion" really means, this test has been used to stamp out even the mildest of nods from the government to the good of religion as an aspect of the common good of society.

This consequence leads, then, to a discussion of the third norm from *Dignitatis humanae,* perhaps the one marking the deepest rift with current Supreme Court doctrine. The bishops at the Second Vatican Council asserted that governments have a duty to take account of and to foster the religious lives of their people, since religion is an essential aspect of the good of persons and, therefore, of the common good. The Council taught that

government must fulfill this duty without favoritism or discrimination among various religious organizations and without subjecting anyone to coercion or undue burdens.

The Supreme Court has explicitly rejected this proposal. The
Lemon test will strike down any laws without a "secular purpose,"
or with the primary effect of advancing a religion. Similarly, the
nonendorsement test seeks to weed out any governmental acts
that could be interpreted by a reasonable observer to constitute an
"endorsement" of religion in general. And the noncoercion test,
which sounds like the most rational measure, has been interpreted
so broadly that it forbids the state from subjecting children to sitting quietly while another person speaks a prayer at a noncompul-
sory school event. A state requirement that schools start their day
with "one-minute of silence" was also held to violate the establishment clause, as children might conclude the school wished them
to pray during this minute (*Wallace v. Jaffree,* 1985).

Even those religious expressions in the public square that
have survived such challenges, such as nativity scenes, or prayers
in legislative sessions, or the words "In God we trust" on the
currency, are permitted only because the Court has assured itself
that there is no real religious meaning to these expressions. So a
crèche may be permitted in a city hall so long as it is surrounded
by candy canes, reindeer, and elves to drain any religious meaning from the display.[8] Prayers may be offered at public ceremo-
nies as remnants of "ceremonial deism," as the Court said, to
convey a sense of solemnity and confidence in the future but not
to convey a sense that religion is important or a desirable part of
life.[9] Rote repetition of the phrase "In God we trust" has rendered
it meaningless, and it can therefore be safely printed on currency
and government seals. Prayers at events involving children, how-

ever, are seen as inherently coercive, perhaps because the Court suspects that children lack the capacity of adults to ignore religious meanings that might be implicit in the words spoken.

The pressure to expurgate religion from the public sphere creates a unique set of burdens on religion, since other cultural forces are free to be expressed and advanced in the public sphere and even encouraged by the government. When state limits to religious expression are challenged, believers have found much more protection in the free speech clause of the First Amendment rather than in the free exercise of religion clause. The Court seems determined to give God little chance of being an original voice in public events.

This "nondiscrimination" principle in the Supreme Court's jurisprudence is closely related to the fourth norm in *Dignitatis humanae,* which holds that the essential nature of religious freedom is immunity from state coercion regarding religious beliefs and practices. So long as religions do not threaten public order, the state must refrain from any coercion of believers or religious groups, such as forcing them to engage in activities forbidden by their religion or restraining them from fulfilling their religious duties.

The Supreme Court for a time held a doctrine that seemed to bring it close to this norm by granting some limited protections when a religious believer could demonstrate that a law infringed on his or her free exercise of religion. But in 2004 the Court refused to hear a challenge to a California law that requires Catholic organizations to pay for contraceptive coverage for their employees, regardless of the Church's moral objections to artificial birth control. Similar laws are being adopted around the country, and other states have gone further by seeking to require Catholic hospitals to provide treatments, including abortion, that violate Catholic teaching.

The trend regarding state mandates toward religious organizations is to offer a very narrow statutory exemption from these laws for a subset of such entities, mainly parishes, while requiring all other organizations—religious schools, charities, hospitals, universities—to bow to secular laws and requirements. The argument is that these activities are "secular" in nature, and that the churches engaged in them may not bring their religious beliefs to bear on these properly secular activities. There is a concerted effort on the part of Planned Parenthood, the ACLU, and some labor unions to eliminate Catholic ethical and religious control over Catholic hospitals, charities, nursing homes, and other facilities. If this effort is successful in bringing the courts to tell the Church which of its ministries are Catholic and which are not, then the Catholic Church (along with other religions) will be forbidden to respond to the Lord's command to serve the poor, the sick, and the abandoned in his name. Such laws will not be held to violate the free exercise clause so long as they have no discriminatory purpose. In other words, consistent with the free exercise clause, the state could require hospitals to perform abortions so long as it imposed this requirement on all hospitals.

Even the Supreme Court's nondiscrimination principle has been called into question. In *Locke v. Davey* (2004), the Court upheld a state law that refused a scholarship to a student for the sole reason that the student wished to pursue a degree in theology.[10] All other students were permitted to use their scholarships at any school for any purpose. In other words, the Court approved of a state burden imposed only because of the applicant's religious beliefs. Similarly, the Third Circuit court of appeals held that lawyers could use peremptory challenges to remove jurors who "show a rather consuming propensity to experience the world through a prism of religious beliefs," as demonstrated by devotion to Scripture reading and church attendance.[11] While such burdens may appear trivial, in principle they support the discriminatory exclusion of religious believers and religious organizations from important aspects of civic life.

This effort to eliminate the involvement of religion in public life is a nascent form of state tyranny. Napoleon and Lenin accomplished the same goal more directly, by simply decreeing that the Church could only run worship services inside parish churches while banning other kinds of religious activity and the involvement of religious institutions in the culture at large. The current U.S. effort is more indirect, leaving the semblance of a choice as to whether the Church will accept state control in contravention of its moral teachings, but it is no less insidious.

This trend presents a challenge to the fifth and last norm from *Dignitatis humanae,* requiring the state to permit religious organizations to create and govern entities in pursuit of their goals of education, charity, and care for the poor and vulnerable. These organizations are important, vitally important, and not only for enabling religious believers to express their belief in efforts on behalf of those who are most in need. In many of our inner cities and rural communities, the only institutions offering health care, shelters, safe schools, and social services are run by churches or other religious bodies. Thirty-one percent of medical care in the state of Illinois, for example, is provided by Catholic hospitals, and much of that is in the poorest parts of the state. Churches challenge social injustices through their efforts on behalf of the suffering, the poor, and the needy. It is significant that these religious groups are not only burdened by an establishment clause jurisprudence that makes nondiscriminatory access to government funds problematic; religious groups are also increasingly threatened by the withdrawal of free exercise protections when state mandates burden the religious beliefs motivating their public works. The combined impact of these First Amendment doctrines is muted by the fact that they come out in dribs and drabs as controversies make their way to the Supreme Court and doctrines take shape and mutate over time. This process doesn't present a consistent approach to limiting the free exercise of religion and forbidding God to act in public life. But limiting it is.

These examples amount to a failure to acknowledge and protect vital elements of religious liberty. Supreme Court doctrine, while offering many important religious protections, has in practice rejected other aspects of each of the key norms proposed by *Dignitatis humanae*. The Court's interpretation of the First Amendment refuses to acknowledge either explicitly or implicitly that religious liberty is rooted in human dignity itself and is oriented toward the attainment of religious truths that can be publicly argued. The Court would seem to deny that the state should foster religion as an aspect of the common good, should refrain from any coercion in religious matters unless necessary for the maintenance of public order, and should permit religions to create and govern organizations in conformity with their beliefs, unless it can be shown that these religious organizations are operating in a profanely secular universe and on its antireligious terms.

The path upon which the Supreme Court has placed our culture does not offer great hope that religious liberty will expand to its fullest possible meaning in law or become more deeply rooted in our culture. The trends point, rather, to a First Amendment doctrine that permits government to further limit the ability of religious believers to live out their commitments fully in public life and opens up further threats that the state may burden and discriminate against religious practices and even eliminate the existence of religiously governed organizations, except in the narrowest sense. Should these trends be placed into concrete laws, religious believers would be forced to decide upon their primary loyalty, whether to God or to Caesar. It is supremely unhealthy for a culture to create such dilemmas and consequently alienate citizens who are religious believers. Our culture should steer clear of these rifts and their dangers to our social coherence.

Finally, we should recall that churches and religious believers owe corresponding duties under a correct understanding of religious liberty: to live in conformity to the truth, to educate and form people who will build up a society that respects the full dignity of the human person, and to witness boldly so that others may share in the light of truth. Churches themselves can contribute to religious liberty by continuing these missions regardless of the legal or constitutional doctrines that prevail at any particular moment. All believers are called to cooperate with those who profess no religion in the search for common good, on the basis of a sound relation between faith and reason. Legal cultures come and go, and the Church has lived through times of favor and times of persecution here and in other parts of the world. With regard to the future of religious liberty, members of the Catholic community can pledge to continue their efforts to live up to their duties as believers and to contribute, because of their faith, to the building up of a sane and healthy society. It would be good, however, to do all of this constitutionally and explicitly in cooperation with a provident God and in his name.

3

PERSONAL FREEDOM
IN AMERICAN CULTURE:
WE CAN'T ACT IF GOD CAN'T

A little more than a century ago, Oliver Wendell Holmes took up a task something like the one I would like to pursue here. On January 8, 1897, Holmes dedicated a new law school building and took the measure of law and culture at the turn of a century. He spoke at Boston University, and his lecture was published as "The Path of the Law." It has become a classic of legal literature.

Holmes placed before his audience the proposition that "the man of the future is the man of statistics and the master of economics."[1] While I do not belittle statistics and economics or deny their importance to the law, I wish to reflect on fundamental *moral* truths, truths that are by nature irreducible to numbers and resistant to calculation. Further, Holmes greeted not only a new century but also the dawn of a truly *national* culture. He knew as well as anyone the world that was slipping away: an America of isolated communities, of regional if not local cultures, of a vigorous and more than occasionally strident ethnicity. Deep cultural and legal divisions drew Holmes's blood at the Battle of

Antietam; he was wounded three times in that great crucible of national bonding, the Civil War. He was preparing to set the course of law for a new culture in a different age.

The experience of fratricidal war transformed Holmes's character. Without television or radio or anything approaching a national press and without a national consumer market to homogenize the country, Americans were as different, region to region, ethnic group to ethnic group, as inhabitants of different countries are today. Those differences would not be significantly domesticated until the Second World War united diverse Americans in a single national purpose. In many ways that great conflict completed the job begun by the Civil War: the forging of a singular American cultural identity. Holmes stood that January day of 1897 in Boston on the verge of the only world contemporary Americans have known, a world of huge cities, instant communication, an integrated national economy, a large, highly bureaucratized federal government, a truly national culture. Ours is a world in which all levels of government mold the warp and woof of daily life to an extent unimaginable to our nation's Founders and even to those who reconstructed the nation after the Civil War.

We stand now at the dawn of still another age, the age of globalization, of an economy without borders, of international law and world culture, all carried by the Internet, cell phones, satellite television, and jet travel. Ours is the world of the United Nations, the euro, and high school field trips to Kenya. The globalization of culture has already had an impact on law, chiefly by dramatically reducing any government's control over culture and thus over people's habits and beliefs. This curtailment creates critical challenges worthy of the most careful reflection, and I will turn now to consider more carefully the equally critical question of the central role and ongoing task of law in the formation of American culture.

"Culture," broadly understood, is the world that people in a given society make by what they do and why they do it. It is a human artifact brought into being by the practices and habits of a people, especially their purposive activity. "Culture" thus reflects and is shaped by people's understandings of meaning and value. No culture can be critically understood except by probing people's ends, their goals; their beliefs about what is good and bad, right and wrong, just and unjust, noble and base; their understanding of the ultimate source or sources of meaning and value; their relationship to God. It is especially the hierarchy of values, the relative importance of each of the goods present in every authentically human culture, that defines a culture's particularity, its genius. It is true that the positive sciences of culture (anthropology, sociology, parts of political science) strive to bracket ultimate questions, including questions of moral truth, for the sake of accurate description. But the concept of culture is not necessarily relativistic; speaking of culture as an autonomous human artifact does not imply moral relativism. People make cultures, and they characteristically make them according to what they believe God or the gods wish of them. People make cultures, in other words, according to what they believe is true. And we can judge their efforts by reference to the truth, as we are given to understand it.

Christians believe that culture must ultimately be judged by reference to the fullness of truth in Christ. This does not mean Christian faith supposes that there is some single uniquely correct culture. There is a legitimately wide range of cultural variability, circumscribed only by basic principles of justice and charity and other fundamental and universal moral truths. The Second Vatican Council called for a dialogue between faith and culture, a conversation that is successor to the earlier legal conversation between Church and state. In our culture, that dialogue must include a conversation between faith, which is one normative system, and the law, which is another.

When American law was mostly common law, as it was when Holmes addressed his Boston listeners, its relationship to culture was harmonious, because the law was almost wholly derivative from the culture. The common law was conceived of as the distillation of shared practice, of culturally common activities. The law was not any judge's say-so or even the say-so of the judiciary as a body; judicial declarations counted, rather, as so much evidence of the law. The law remained the common practices of the people, discerned more or less adequately by judges but not made or determined by them.

Holmes recognized this relation between common law and the people's moral beliefs and practices. But he provocatively urged his listeners to come to understand laws on radically different terms: as predictions of what courts will do rather than reflections of what the people commonly do. Laws for Holmes were prophecies made from what he famously called the perspective of the "bad man."[2] The "bad man" does not treat legal rules as reasons for his actions; he cares not a whit for their moral rightness or wrongness. His concern, rather, is with their consequences for his possible *future* actions. For him, the rules of law are mere integers in an equation whose sum supplies valuable data about the potential unpleasant consequences of pursuing this goal as opposed to that.

We live in an age of statutes, administrative rules, executive

orders, treaties, and judicial decisions conceived differently—
more creatively and more like legislation—than was the common
law. Law characteristically is, for us, the purposive ordering of
norms, first imagined, debated, and then given life, once and for
all, on a certain date, down at city hall, up in the statehouse, or in
a court in Washington, D.C. All these forms of law, these enact-
ments, bind by dint of someone's or some institution's authority,
not by dint of prior custom and practice. The modern relationship between law and culture is therefore fragile, more complex
and problematic.

Bearing this complexity in mind, let us now look at law from
the perspective not of Holmes's "bad man" but rather of the good
and conscientious citizen, one who is eager to act in conformity
to God's purposes and action in the world. From this vantage
point, the central challenge in thinking about law and culture
may be likened to resolving the paradox of the chicken and the
egg. In the face of unjust and immoral practices, some well-
intentioned people look immediately and single-mindedly to law
to "solve" the problem. They see legislation as the primary cure
for moral defects. "There ought to be a law," they say. Viewing
law as the engine driving the cultural train, they fail to see that
cultural reform and renewal usually require much work beyond
the domain of law. On account of this failure, their efforts at reform frequently stall and, even when they partially succeed,
breed disrespect for laws that are perceived as "out of touch"
with reality, unenforceable, ineffective. The fact that the legal
prohibition of alcoholic beverages had to be repealed by constitutional amendment is one example.

Other good people fall into the opposite error. They are
often too complacent in the face of evil cultural practices or

intimidated by the power or prestige of forces supporting them. They view laws as mere epiphenomena of culture. "You can't legislate morality" is their slogan. "We should forgo the pursuit of legal justice," they say, "until people are brought round to accept a sound moral understanding" of whatever matter is at hand. They place all their hopes for reform and renewal in "education" and other extralegal efforts in the cultural sphere. When it comes to the sanctity of life, for example, they insist that it is only by changing people's hearts, not by reforming the laws, that unborn children can be protected against the violence of abortion.

Many used to say this about racial justice. This proposition figured prominently in the argument made in 1954 by John W. Davis, the great Supreme Court advocate (and loser of the 1924 presidential election) in his defense of school segregation laws in *Brown v. Board of Education*. Davis allowed that segregation might be unjust and, as an initial matter, courts might rather have held that it was unconstitutional. But in earlier cases courts had not so ruled; instead, courts, including the Supreme Court, consistently said that "separate but equal" satisfied all relevant constitutional requirements. So, Davis observed, an entire culture had been built upon segregation. It would be foolish and counterproductive, he suggested, to try to uproot this entire culture by changing the law. Legal reform would have to be put on hold until more favorable cultural conditions came into being. Law would have to follow culture: "You can't legislate morality."

The Court, to its credit, rejected this argument. The justices in *Brown* struck a ringing blow for justice in the face of a culture corroded by the acid of racism. Of course, it is true that a judicial decree does not, by itself, convert anyone's heart. And the Court's writ in *Brown* did not run very far, very fast. But "all deliberate speed" is neither neutral nor reverse, however much we may be eager to move into high gear. The *Brown* Court knew that law, whether just or unjust, functions as a teacher. It is capable of instigating great cultural change, and it is capable of profoundly reinforcing a status quo. The justices knew that segregation, as a cultural practice, would not end so long as law testified, and thus taught, in season and out, that black and white are unequal. The Court fell into neither of the two errors I mentioned, believing that legal reform is sufficient to overcome social evils or supposing that such reform has no significant role in social change.

The laws invalidated by the Supreme Court in *Brown* were, in the beginning, effects of racism rather than its causes. Segregation manifested cultural prejudices, the widespread belief among whites that blacks were inferior. But does anyone doubt for a second that legally required segregation—with blacks being consigned to quarters on the far side of the tracks, drinking from "colored only" water fountains, and traipsing past whites to the rear of the bus—reinforced, perpetuated, and, over time, helped to create that culture? Discriminatory laws structured a world of difference, a universe demarcated by color, which confronted its inhabitants as an ineradicable fact, a given, like a force of nature, for a culture is second nature to those who live in it. People, both black and white, tended to internalize the norms of laws protecting patterns of racial segregation. The law called forth the ideology by which racism was defended, thus rationalizing and deepening the bias that brought it into being. Segregation laws grew out of prejudice, but they also perpetuated it. Without the edifice of segregation and other Jim Crow laws, the ideology of racism would have atrophied, as, mercifully, it seems to be doing today.

Another flaw in Davis's argument is this: in questions of basic human rights, appeals to culture count for very little. Equal protection of the law is a basic human right, rooted in the equal dignity of all human persons. Those exercising public authority bear a particular, though not unique, responsibility to establish justice, a responsibility, incidentally, denied by Justice Holmes. That Holmes himself or even the majority of those whom public authorities serve and represent happened subjectively to prefer what is objectively unjust alters this responsibility not at all. On matters of fundamental justice, even conscientious opposition to what is objectively right must be resolutely resisted and overcome. There were, no doubt, advocates of slavery and segregation who conscientiously believed in the inferiority of black persons and thus in the justice of these monstrous practices. Those who saw these evils for what they were, however, were right to impose the truth upon racists, however sincere the racists may have been.

Now, if the Supreme Court got the relationship between law and culture right in the case of segregation, it got it tragically wrong on the issue of abortion. In the 1992 case *Planned Parenthood v. Casey,* which reaffirmed the right to abortion created ex nihilo almost twenty years earlier in *Roe v. Wade,* the plurality opinion of Justices O'Connor, Kennedy, and Souter suggested that one or more of the justices in the *Casey* majority would, as an initial matter, have decided *Roe* differently. But now it was too late. Some of these justices were concerned about the prestige of the Court and said much about why overruling *Roe* at this late date would damage that prestige. But why? And what made the date too late?

The answer to both questions is clear. It is, in form, John

W. Davis's argument from *Brown*. The justices in *Casey* say that a generation of "people have organized intimate relationships and made choices that define their views of themselves and their places in society, in reliance on the availability of abortion."[3] The stakes were, assertedly, highest for women: "The ability of women to participate equally in the economic and social life of the Nation has been facilitated by their ability to control their reproductive lives."[4] Abortion guarantees that liberty, the justices asserted, and that equal participation.

Is this not to say that legal abortion is the linchpin of our culture, at least of women's role in it? Is a more powerful testimony to law's power to create, or to destroy, a culture imaginable? If so, and also in light of *Brown,* do we not have to attribute to law a culture-forming capacity at odds with the anthem of recent liberal political theory, which demands that government remain steadfastly neutral about "the good," about what counts as genuine human flourishing?

In fact, the comparison to *Brown* is tighter than one might think. In that earlier case, the justices were squarely confronted with a conflict between the requirements of justice and the practices of a culture. But attorneys in *Roe* also clearly presented the Court with arguments about the requirements of justice, arguments about the injustice of abortion to unborn human beings, arguments that implied the constitutional necessity of substantial restrictions on feticide: if the unborn are "persons," their right to life is guaranteed by the Constitution. The *Roe* Court did not accept these arguments, and since then the only standing alternative to the permissive regime affirmed in *Casey* has been a fallback to federalism: the U.S. Constitution, being allegedly "silent" about abortion, consigns the matter to fifty state legislatures. But the Constitution is *not* silent. The Constitution expressly protects the right of all "persons" to the equal protection of the laws, including the laws against homicide. If, as science discloses, philosophy argues, and faith confirms, unborn human beings are "persons," then their rights, too, are protected. Competent jurists and constitutional scholars disagree about the respective roles of Congress and the federal courts in enforcing the equal protection clause and other Fourteenth Amendment guarantees, but there is no escaping the question of the constitutional rights of the unborn.

Law and culture stand in a complex dialectical relationship. Neither comes first; neither comes last. Law contributes massively to the formation of culture; culture influences and shapes law. Inescapably, inevitably, law and culture stand in a mutually informing, formative, and reinforcing relationship. For this reason and many others, the liberal ideal of governmental "neutrality" on contested cultural-moral issues, allegedly leaving everyone "free" to pursue their own private visions of the good and thus attain personal fulfillment, is an illusion. Either it amounts to nonsense or it masks an ideology of social engineering.

It is simply not possible for law to be "morally neutral" on abortion. The law since *Roe v. Wade* is certainly not neutral. It embodies very definite, controversial, and manifestly false beliefs about the rights and dignity of the unborn child. However firmly Justice Blackmun in his opinion in that case insisted that the justices were taking no position on the question "when life begins," the effect of their ruling was to decide just that question, and to decide it in a way that comports neither with the scientific evidence nor with sound philosophical analysis. Moreover, the lessons taught by the law's denial of the humanity and equal dignity of the child are anything but neutral; they are tragic. What woman feeling pressure to have an abortion not only from her social or economic circumstances but perhaps also from a boyfriend, husband, or parent will not be tempted to think: "Abortion cannot be killing a developing human being; for if it were, then the law would prohibit it"? Law, in this instance, stifles the voice of conscience, the grace of God.

It is true, of course, that our law compels no woman to have an abortion, but that is no evidence of neutrality. Did the fact that the laws of South Carolina in 1859 compelled no one to own slaves mean that the law of that state was "neutral" on the question of slavery? Would we for a moment credit the claim of a supporter of slave laws to be merely "pro-choice" rather than pro-slavery? Would we accept a pro-slavery politician's assurances that he is "personally opposed" to the practice? Those Catholic politicians and others who today consistently support pro-abortion laws while claiming to be personally opposed to abortion ought to reflect on the ignominy in which Roger Brooke Taney, the author of the Supreme Court's tragic pro-slavery decision in the 1857 case *Dred Scott v. Sandford,* is held. Taney was a Catholic from Maryland who actually freed his own slaves. He was "personally opposed." Yet his support for the right of others to own slaves and to take their slaves into free territory makes us ashamed today. But on the logic of those who today rationalize their support for legal abortion, he was merely "pro-choice."

When it comes to abortion, euthanasia, and other sanctity of life issues, we should not suppose that our choice is between reforming the law and working to change the culture. We must do both. The work of legal reform is a necessary, though not sufficient, ingredient in the larger project of cultural transformation. Yes, we must change people's hearts. But no, we must not wait for changes of heart before changing the laws. We must do both at the same time, recognizing that just laws help to form good hearts, and unjust laws impede every other effort in the cause of the Gospel of Life. Teaching and preaching that gospel, reaching out in love and compassion to pregnant women in need, all of this "cultural" work is indispensable and mandated for one who strives, with the help of God, to bring life out of death. Without it, we will never effect legal reform or, if we do, the laws will not bear the weight we will be assigning to them. But even as these endeavors go forward, we need to work tirelessly for the legal protection of the right to life of the unborn child. It is not either/or, law or culture; it is both/and. Efforts in each sphere presuppose and depend upon the success of efforts in the other.

Consider other areas where law, culture, and religious norms interact. The realm of marriage and family life is obviously one. The laws of every society are crucial in establishing the concrete conditions under which people come to be and are brought to maturity. Laws surrounding marriage and family can strengthen or weaken the integrity and vitality of a community. Yet in the name of individual "privacy," "autonomy," and "freedom," important protections of family life have been erased from the law. And many, especially in the most affluent and highly educated sectors of American life, have apparently persuaded themselves that the erasure of these laws results in greater individual freedom. But studies now prove otherwise.

In the area of economic life, the absence of law does not necessarily advance freedom and may often contract it. The 1905 case *Lochner v. New York* has come to epitomize the Supreme

Court's early failure to understand this fact. In *Lochner,* the justices struck down a law preventing the exploitation of laborers who were subjected to excessive working hours in potentially hazardous conditions. Justice Holmes dissented from this opinion, not because the Court was failing to protect human rights but because he believed it should tailor the law to contemporary social developments. The fact that this decision is today an embarrassment to the Supreme Court and, like *Dred Scott,* a blot on its record reflects a more sober judgment of the ways in which the laissez-faire philosophy it stands for provided a mask for economic oppression.

The lesson should be clear, and it clearly applies to cultural life beyond the domain of the marketplace: when law retreats, all one can say for sure is that individuals are "free" to confront the nonlegal structures of society, an often unforgiving system of unregulated exchange that may invite the exploitation of labor in the vacuum previously inhabited by a proper legal care for public morality. The law's retreat from economic life may very well leave upright persons, families, and institutions of civil society vulnerable to a massive, objective framework of settled understandings and expectations, a culture that, though it is destructive and debilitating, the poor lack effective resources to resist. For those who can and do resist, there may well be at least informal sanctions and penalties of ostracism, rejection, and stigma.

Even by its absence, therefore, law can shape culture in destructive ways. The law's refusal to interfere with the institution of slavery helped to establish and maintain a culture corrupted by an ideology of racial superiority and inferiority. The law's refusal to protect unborn children similarly shapes and hardens a culture that, corroded by the treatment of unborn human beings as "nonpersons," places in jeopardy the right to life of any group that loses political clout.

It is simply a myth to suppose that the retreat of law necessarily enhances freedom. The cultural structures people sometimes face in the absence of law can leave them anything but "free." Is one's teenage daughter truly "free" to engineer her own pattern of courtship? Can she call forth a corresponding attitude on the parts of the young men who are potentially eligible to her as boyfriends? How "free" is she to be the chaste young woman she should be and her parents want her to be? Would she not be freer in a world in which accepted understandings and expectations supported, rather than hindered, her natural desire to be treated with dignity by young men who present themselves to her as possible romantic partners? Don't the laws against rape serve to make her free?

Marriage is a social institution, one that confronts us with a more or less established set of expectations and understandings. What the legal political philosopher Joseph Raz says of monogamy applies to all of the constitutive features of marriage (sexual exclusivity, heterosexuality, permanence of commitment) and even to courtship patterns: "Monogamy, assuming that it is the only valuable form of marriage, cannot be practiced by an individual. It requires a culture which recognizes it, and which supports it through the public's attitude and through its formal institutions."[5] The upshot of Professor Raz's observation is that large numbers of people are not effectively free to enter into monogamous marriages unless the culture makes the institution of marriage constituted as monogamous available to people. And the further implication is that law has an essential, though subsidiary, role in establishing and maintaining a healthy culture of court-ship and marriage.

Until a generation or so ago, all this was taken for granted. Courts, legislatures, legal scholars, and people in general long agreed that marriage is a public institution with its own na-ture, protected in significant measure by legal norms settled upon in conformity with that nature. In the words of a late nineteenth-century Supreme Court opinion: "[Marriage is] an institution, in the maintenance of which in its purity the public is deeply interested, for it is the foundation of the family and of society, without which there would be neither civilization nor progress."[6]

But what is it about marriage that is "public"? Which fea-tures of the complex and dynamic unity we call married life are selected and settled by political authority and taken under public guardianship? Surely it is not the whole, or even most, of mar-riage. Law can hardly control the ordinary give-and-take be-tween spouses or dictate the terms of their daily efforts to live together in harmony and conjugal love. Most of what goes on in any marriage is not susceptible to legal regulation or subject to sanction. The economic life of the couple, for example, is public business only at the edges. We no longer impose an economic template upon married people, assigning wholesale to the wife a dependent, inferior economic existence. And our law, including our constitutional law, has long protected the liberty of spouses and, in that sense, their "privacy" with respect to sexual inti-macy and their personal right "to direct the upbringing and ed-ucation of their children."[7] For better or worse, the law does not even restrict the use or availability of contraceptive methods of family planning. In the 1965 case *Griswold v. Connecticut,* the Supreme Court ruled that no attempt to do so could comport with a right of what the justices called "marital privacy."[8]

Still the courts, even in *Griswold,* affirm that marriage is inherently social and necessarily protected and governed by norms put into place by public authority. In 1948, Justice Robert Jackson spoke for the Court in another case: "If there is one thing that the people are entitled to expect from their law-makers, it is rules of law that will enable individuals to tell whether they are married and, if so, to whom . . . the uncertain-ties that result [from legal ambiguity] are not merely technical, nor are they trivial: the lawfulness of their cohabitation, their children's legitimacy, their title to property, and even whether they are law-abiding persons or criminals."[9]

In 1961, Justice John Harlan, though writing in support of the result achieved four years later in *Griswold,* said, "The laws regarding marriage . . . provide both when the sexual powers may be used and the legal and societal context in which children are born and brought up, as well as laws forbidding adultery, fornication and homosexual practice, which express the negative of that proposition."[10] Putting aside Jackson's reference to prop-erty titles, we have here testimony that both of the central as-pects of marriage stand vitally in need of the protections of law: the unitive aspect of marriage in chaste sexual congress and the procreative aspect of marriage. Since we have spent the last thirty years "privatizing" sexual conduct and procreation, removing them from legal specification, the "privatization" of marriage is likewise advancing. Public discourse not only debates whether homosexual liaisons can be called marriage but is also open to other patterns of sexual activity being included under the rubric. A marriage is what those who want to marry say it is.

Exploiting the public conversation and appealing to the logic of earlier Court decisions, advocates of same-sex "marriage" have come to courts demanding, in the name of "equality," the redefinition of marriage to accommodate homosexual partnerships. Such a move would obliterate, at a stroke, the traditional conception of marriage in our law and culture as a one-flesh union of sexually complementary spouses ordered to the generation, nurture, and education of children. It would remove any logical basis for insisting on monogamy, fidelity, or permanence of marital commitment. Effectively, it would abolish the already bruised and battered institution of marriage in our culture. Consequently, many believe that the best way to save marriage from privatization and effective abolition in our culture is for pro-family forces to unite across denominational and racial lines to work for a federal constitutional amendment to protect marriage from judicial redefinition.

Culture does not exist in a legal vacuum, as if there is, or could be, some pure culture, defined as what happens without law. Law is necessary to civilization, and even the absence of law, the choice to omit or remove legal regulation in some area of cultural life, shapes culture, for better or for worse. Apart from the most doctrinaire libertarians, no one believes that the unregulated market yields pure economic freedom; nor should anyone imagine that the retreat of the law from family life and related areas of culture yields personal liberation or fulfillment. Injustice and oppression can certainly come from the presence of laws that should not exist, but they can also result from the absence of laws that should. Outlaws are, by definition, less than civilized.

The thesis pursued here is that civil law must, for the sake of human flourishing, enter into a more creative partnership with the cultural institutions of marriage, family, and religion. These institutions have legal status for the simple reason that law exists for the people whose well-being and flourishing are dependent upon their being protected. Marriage, family, and religion do not exist for the law or for public polity or for the success of the nation-state as an actor on the world historical scene, or for the growth of the gross national product. Things are the other way around. The moral purpose and justification of law itself are to support the institutions of civil society, of civil culture, for the sake of the common good. That's a philosophical statement, and therefore the law itself can't judge it; one has to step outside the law to make such an evaluation. But it is a very human and cultural statement, inasmuch as it says that the law is to be judged by its fostering of the common good. The moral purpose and justification for law is its support of the institutions of civil society for the sake of the common good of the persons who are shaped by that society's culture.

The proper ordering, therefore, of law and the institutions of civil society is possible only when the civil law maker understands and accepts what is true about these institutions, respects the properties that are theirs before they become the objects of law or its subjects in jurisprudence, and knows why and how these institutions are part of the good life for all peoples. When this moral understanding is lacking, it's very hard to have intelligent promotion and regulation of marriage, family, and religion. The weakening of these institutions, no longer buttressed by law, or even their destruction because of poor jurisprudence, has long-term cultural consequences and, therefore, consequences for the human beings caught up in a profoundly defective culture.

This sense of the interplay of law and the cultural institutions it should protect and foster creates a political institution, a state that is committed equally to the well-being of everyone. The state and its laws are for the perfection of human beings, families, and associations. A corollary to this understanding of the social and political order is the principle of subsidiarity, according to which the state fulfills its high purpose by not substituting itself for the initiative and responsibility of individuals, or of intermediate communities at the level at which they can function. Arguing that law is a necessary instrument for the common good doesn't mean that law has to stipulate all of the details of action by the individuals and institutions that it is supposed to protect. Distinctions among public institutions and social activities are obvious.

At one end of the spectrum are those cultural institutions that are almost wholly the creatures of law. Although these organizations maintain a certain formal autonomy, they depend upon the natural virtues of sociability, honesty, and fairness. They serve the common good in a malleable manner. The courts, the jury system, electoral colleges, most corporations are simply means to ends. They can be transformed fairly much at will, sometimes with the result that they no longer serve the common good. Elections that produce no clear winners or invariably award offices to miserable candidates are elections that don't work, so the electoral system should be changed by law. The lawmaker's task in these cases is simple to comprehend, though often difficult to achieve: to devise a better system to deliver the desired end, staying within the bounds of morality and not sacrificing justice for efficiency. But that's not to say there's only one way to construct a legal system or only one way to conduct an election.

At the other end of the spectrum are practices and institutions that work without the law's jump start, and they flourish without the law's help. Friendship and neighborhood, most of culture as it is often understood—the high culture of the arts and literature—are beyond the notice of law and should be. Ordinary promises outside the special area of commercial contracts are also outside the governance of the law itself. So is the daily give-and-take of family life. Spouses who ignore each other and children who don't clean their rooms are not about to be hauled before a civil magistrate to give an account of their derelictions, at least not in a democratic and free society.

In the middle are to be found the hardest and yet the most important cases of the interrelationship between law and culture. Public authority enters into partnership with cultural institutions and activities that it does not create or initiate but that it nevertheless officially recognizes and regulates, promotes, supports, protects. The contemporary moral philosopher John Finnis puts it this way: "The law supervenes upon these cultural institutions and by so doing creates within limits a legal version or a dimension of a particular social practice or institution."[11] These are the areas where law and morality most obviously are joined and where public discussions about religious influence on law and public life become acrimonious because different forms of relationships have been historically instantiated.

Institutions that mark every society, like marriage, family life, economic activity, and religious service, have their own history of state supervision; but even more illustrative of the way law and culture interact are the activities that were more or less consensual and once were legally approved but are now prohibited: dueling is prohibited, as are vendettas, prostitution rings, known networks for the consensual exchange of sex with minors, humiliating initiation rites. This kind of legislation recognizes that society is not just a collection of autonomous individuals with their particular subjective criteria determining moral issues. Lawmakers therefore often work against what many people want and desire. For many years the whole edifice of public moral laws concerning lewdness and obscenity depended upon recognition of the destructive power of unrestrained sexual desire and its consequent moral hazards. Numerous laws came into being to protect marriage from subversion by extramarital relations, which tempt many individuals. For example, the drive for cloning human embryos to be used in biomedical research and involving their deliberate destruction is fueled by the worthy desire to find cures for Alzheimer's, Parkinson's, and other diseases—good ends, which obscure for many the evil means involved. It is not paternalistic on the part of the state but realistic to recognize the fragility of persons in the face of certain powerful temptations of fallen human nature. Sometimes it is unjust not to protect persons against these very forces in themselves.

The highest form of human association is not the legal community, the national community, the cultural community; it is the community that unites us to the God who acts for our well-being here and who desires our eternal salvation. The political good, while limited in scope, can nevertheless be instrumental in achieving a higher goal, in acting for a higher purpose. A good society forms good people and appreciates the help of religious institutions in this social objective. A bad society pulls people back into themselves, without higher purpose or destiny. The interaction between the Catholic Church and the state is tense in this country not just because the state sometimes regards any purposes higher than its own objectives as distractions but also because the Church maintains her unique sense of herself as a visible society instituted by Christ. Her public structures and forms of governance predate the formation of the modern nation-state. This fact gives rise to the accusation that the Catholic Church wants to be a state within the State.

If the structures of the Church were not themselves part of the content of faith, then the only public law, even for the Church, would be civil law. The Catholic Church, however, has always insisted that civil law is not the highest law. There is divine law, and, as a visible society, the Church also maintains her own set of laws. While this position is sometimes resented, the purpose of the civil society is to assist people to perfect themselves by properly promoting their various associations and then leaving them free to be faithful, according to a higher law. Cooperation between Church and state is therefore necessary in the creation of good civil laws.

If the law is creating a nonsustainable culture, being used to destroy rather than protect, then Catholics and others engaged in shaping the law are called to engage in an activity of vast importance. Tocqueville pointed out that lawyers are the aristocracy in our form of federal republic. They carry the culture and they work for all of us so that law is not reduced to a mere forum for refereeing individual disputes. If the law does not properly serve the common good, then it's particularly important for Catholics and other believers to take stock of the situation, to recognize the forces that are pulling us in wrong directions, and to defend the sanctity of life, the dignity of marriage, and the freedom of religion from this kind of legal assault. We can deliberately and self-consciously work to reform our culture, with the help of God.

This chapter began with the assertion that Justice Oliver Wendell Holmes helped to set American law on the wrong path a century ago in separating law from morality and truth, leaving law the plaything of forces purely political or the object of manipulation by pressure groups. I argued that, if Catholic faith and American culture are to dialogue, the law's relation to culture in the United States must be appreciated, for law is the primary carrier of culture in this pluralistic society; law is the forger of our national identity and of our collective sense of right and wrong. The intersection between law and morality is therefore a crucial point in the dialogue between faith and culture.

In that intersection, what can law do? Alone, it cannot cure moral defects in a people. It can, however, change people's sense of their hierarchy of values and of what finally falls out of the realm of acceptable behavior. In working to create a culture open to the transcendent truths of faith, therefore, Catholic jurists, legislators, and voters should intend to shape a legal system informed by a sense of right and wrong that is resistant to political manipulation. In this, they work in cooperation with God, who wants his people to be protected by law in order to be free to act.

4

Freedom and Truth: Cooperating with God

A God who acts freely creates men and women, human beings who participate in the gift of life by acting freely. If we are to cooperate actively with God, then the connection between acting freely and knowing the truth has to be explored. If trapped in falsehood, human acting will prevent cooperation with a God who is truth. Given at least some external legal protection for religious freedom, what are the bases for freedom that are intrinsic to the human person?

The philosophical bases traced in this chapter are of two sorts. One outlook reduces a human person to an individual who is established by choices rooted in will, an autonomous being for whom relationships get in the way. A movie star of my youth, Greta Garbo, was famous for her line "I want to be alone." Many chuckled at her solemn intonation of the statement because they instinctively knew that wanting to be completely alone is a death wish.

The other philosophy bases human personhood on what the Church and many others maintain as essential to decent human living: family and friends, love itself, virtue, country, art, and the spiritual life. If all of these components are sacrificed in order to base personhood on autonomous will, then the primary cultural imperative is to control the world, often using sophisticated technological means. To assure his or her humanity, a person must see to it that everything comes out exactly as he or she wills it to. In that kind of culture, which is more and more our kind of culture, there is an obsession with risk. More and more of the economic resources of our society are given to legal claims, insurance costs, and security. When the ability to control events now and in the future finally fails, the economy itself will be exhausted, and we will be economically bankrupt as well as morally spent. We will be living in a prison of our own making, because we have ceased to rely on and cooperate with the providence of God.

In contrast with the autonomous person, defined by choices based only on individual desire, without reference to anything except the will itself, there is another sense of person grounded in both faith and reason. A person is established in a network of relationships that are given, first of all, by God and discovered, first of all, in families. These are relationships that, over a lifetime, people grow into, slowly disengaging themselves from selfishness in order to become totally free to give themselves generously without worrying about the risk. When the chips are down, when there is a failure of human initiative and endeavor, then it is the language of self-sacrifice that makes sense and explains who human persons truly are. Recall how, with the destruction of the *Columbia* space shuttle in 2003, when not only the mission into space but human life itself was lost, people reached spontaneously for the vocabulary of self-sacrifice. At a memorial service on January 31, 1986, for the seven astronauts who perished in the *Challenger* disaster, President Ronald Reagan said, "Words pale in the shadow of grief; they seem insufficient even to measure the brave sacrifice of those you loved and we so admired." By speaking of the tragedy in these terms, the president gave significance to what was otherwise a total failure.

How can we know what the human person is and is called to be? Believers know it from faith; we walk in that light. But everyone can also know it by human reason. We know it, each of us in different ways, according to our individual histories of grace and the personal human dynamic that has shaped us. A story may help explain what this means in concrete terms.

More than once, I've spoken to gatherings of Rotary International, which has for years dedicated itself to the eradication of polio in the world. This service organization has given enormous amounts of money and time, so that now there are only a few countries left where there is still childhood polio. In those remote places, especially since there is almost no possibility of postpolio care—operations and braces and guided exercise—the effects of the disease can be eradicated only by prevention. Rotary has become a principal instrument for seeing that this happens. Out of gratitude to them, since I had polio myself, I have sometimes talked about my experience. I won't go into the experience of the disease itself for a thirteen-year-old boy. I want only to draw from it two points that have shaped my search for God's activity in the context of a debilitating and sometimes deadly disease.

The first point is that a person is never an object. I learned this when being treated in a teaching hospital in Chicago. At that time, they brought a patient on a gurney into an amphitheater where all the medical students stared down at you. Your name was never mentioned; you were never introduced. Perhaps that small recognition of human subjectivity would have gotten in the way of the lessons that the doctors wanted to teach to medical students. But, young though I was, I knew something was radically wrong in that situation. A human person is more than an object for inspection. No matter the need for objective learning, a human subject is more than a mere instrument to advance scientific knowledge. At the time, I did not judge that something was morally wrong, still less was I able to conclude that something was philosophically wrong. Jean-Paul Sartre in *La Nausée* reflects on *le regard*, the stare. He shows how one reduces somebody to an object by staring without recognizing the other as someone whose basic dignity has to be respected, even though various inequalities might remain.

A person is never an object. The popes keep saying that, sometimes invoking the well-known Kantian dictum: a person is always an end, never a means. Perhaps John Paul II came to that recognition early because of the totalitarian society he grew up in. I am convinced of this truth about persons with a conviction beyond philosophical reasoning, which is always open to criticism and argument, because of my personal experience in recovering from polio.

The second conclusion I drew from my experience with physical paralysis was that true freedom is found in coming to terms with limitations, not in imagining that the whole world is going to dispose itself to your will or desires. I have a certain impatience, therefore, with utopian claims and a certain sorrow when I hear a parent tell a child, "You can be anything you want to be." With such a declaration, the child is set up for failure. No one can be anything he or she wants to be. Our will and our desires or dreams don't determine the world. Whether it's God that does, or nature, or just other people, the fact is that a child, in order to succeed, has to learn to live with limitations. I came to that conviction early on because I had good doctors and good parents, who asked me, with a love that echoed God's, what I thought I might do with the gift of my life. How was I to make the best use, as I was trained to walk again, of what I had left of my body? How was I to live without resentment because of what I couldn't do: run, play ball, roller-skate? I very slowly and imperfectly learned a spiritual lesson: to live without resentment is a challenge to faith in a provident God.

It is not only individuals who have to work their way through resentments that come from limitations, whether self-imposed, imposed by others, or imposed by disease or historical tragedy. A whole culture can be born from resentment of the human condition itself. To the extent that there is a utopian claim behind some biotechnological advances, a claim fueled by resentment of the limitations imposed on us by space and time, by death and nature, the culture becomes demonic.

One is led to ask about the roots of such divergent visions of what it means to be human in family and in society. More important, how is dialogue possible so that alliances for common goals can be formed among people who, if left completely alone, recognize they cannot be free? How is a society that is divided on basic questions able to come together around basic truths in order to create a culture of life?

When Karol Wojtyla was working on his major philosophical-anthropological treatise, *Person and Act,* he wrote to Henri de Lubac, "The evil of our times consists in the first place in a kind of degradation, indeed in a pulverization, of the fundamental uniqueness of each human person. This evil is even more of the metaphysical order than of the moral order. To this disintegration, planned at times by atheistic ideologies, we must oppose, rather than sterile polemics, a kind of 'recapitulation' of the inviolable mystery of the person."[1] It is that recapitulation of the inviolable mystery of the person that John Paul II manifested in his concern for dialogue with everyone, whether believers or not.

Because of his conviction that both the Church and the human race need to reestablish the dignity of the human person, John Paul II became in his time the foremost spokesman for the necessity of recognizing human rights and promoting a culture of life, a culture in which human beings can be truly human. Because we are made in God's image and likeness, to be human means to be infinite in our inspired reach even though always finite in our own means. People are able, when they realize their limitations, to turn to God and accept infinity itself, eternity itself, as pure gift. Human subjectivity, which is the locus for our coming to awareness of who we are as people with infinite desires and finite means, is bound up in self-consciousness that is able to discern the spiritual at work in the temporal.

The capacity for self-consciousness that defines us as human beings is related to the self-giving that brings us genuine freedom. I write "capacity" because, if fully evolved self-consciousness is what defines us as human beings, then we run into difficulty in establishing the value of mentally disabled persons. The human being is not just any creature or form of life. Every human being is a person who is capable, although not necessarily very fully, of self-knowledge and self-possession, and therefore capable of freely giving himself and entering into communion with other persons.

That definition is contested by contemporary ethicists like Peter Singer, the Princeton professor who would say that the indicators of personhood are self-awareness, self-control, a sense of the future and past, the capacity to relate to others, concern for others, communication, and curiosity, and all this solely as possessed at any one moment. Personhood is thus not inherent in human individuals but contingent on this development of self-consciousness and its actualization. "I propose," Singer writes, "to use 'person' in the sense of a rational and self-conscious being."[2] The classical question is: what happens then when one is asleep? What is the moral value of someone who has lost consciousness in a coma but whose life can be maintained by mechanical means? Presupposing that people are themselves whether asleep or awake, when unconscious or conscious, means that we recognize the human person as present as a subject with rights from the moment when God creates the spiritual principle or soul that unifies the body, the moment when one is constituted as someone who has a unique bond with his or her Creator. It's not self-consciousness and intelligence that determine personhood but the capacity from nature to develop these powers in some fashion, even though they might be much impeded and differently realized in individual cases. A limited person remains a person, for every human being is limited.

Philosophical tools are needed to grasp this insight properly. What is the explicit relationship between self-consciousness and the freedom that, especially in our culture, enables people to claim to be human? What is the connection between the truth attained by a self-conscious human being and the freedom to give oneself to another or to a great cause? The connection is found when we realize that coming to truths perfects the human person. Most people recognize that truth makes its own objective claim: this is the way things are. When we know that we're thinking about something correctly, we make a truth claim. But if we know the truth about something and, especially, about ourselves, we are not only correctly informed but also better persons; we are better human beings, even in knowing the painful truths about our own limits. Our actions are truly free when, knowing who we are, we act in conformity with the truth that sets us free (Jn 8:32).

John Paul II makes the connection between truth and freedom at the beginning of his encyclical *Fides et ratio* (1998). He quotes the Delphic oracle, "Know thyself." From that command one comes to self-consciousness about who one is as a human person capable of both knowing the truth and freely giving oneself to it and to others. From that ancient command flows the argument about personhood in *Fides et ratio.* The project of coming to know oneself implies an always deepening knowledge of oneself and of one's situation in the world with others. Science and technology can contribute to that basic self-understanding, but, for full self-knowledge by a human person, an excursion into subjectivity cannot be limited to what scientific methodology permits. Knowledge of yourself isn't only knowledge of what you do; it is also knowledge of who you are. The question is not just empirical: How do we come to appear on the scene? How are we in the world with others? Nor is it merely historical: Where have we come from? Nor is it a scientific question: What are we capable of with the help of modern techniques?

Science and technologies can give us answers to all these questions, but the answers are not sufficient until we understand that self-knowledge poses an ethical question: What ought I to do? Purpose then defines who I am. But that also is not the final question. The final question is a metaphysical one: Who are we? Who am I? What is this human person that I believe myself to be? John Paul II puts it in these words: "[The] fundamental elements of knowledge spring from the *wonder* awakened in them [human beings] by the contemplation of creation: Human beings are astonished to discover themselves as part of the world in a relationship to others like them, all sharing a common destiny . . . Without wonder, men and women would lapse into deadening routine and little by little would become incapable of a life which is genuinely personal" (*Fides et ratio,* Introduction). Freedom stands at the beginning of this wonder and the journey into the light of a fuller meaning, which by its very nature has value for the person who is moved by what he has seen and contemplated; it contributes to our completion, our perfection as human beings.

The truth value of my statements is surely measured in their disclosure of what is being discussed, but I am part of the discussion. Our lies, ignorance, faults obscure our knowing. This is especially so of the painful truths about myself that I may try to avoid: that I am lazy or inconsiderate, that I am unable to be an Olympic runner or a bank president, that I have failed to do something important for a friend who has passed away. Truth is especially painful when an unwelcome diagnosis forces me to acknowledge the imminent inevitability of my own death. These are forces, but not forces in the way that natural phenomena are forces, the way a lighted match forces itself into gasoline, for example. On the contrary, it takes courage to push away the evasions and to face the pain. If I have the courage to face even painful situations, I am freed to reach for a solution, to work for peace and justice in ways beyond my own capacities. I feel a certain satisfaction, a liberation, even a certain received fullness in the midst of pain. Truth is not simply "objective." It doesn't merely disclose what is out there apart from me. It is also related to my own being and is, therefore, perfective of who I am. By contrast, if truth claims are reduced to competing opinions that will be settled politically, we will discover the truth only about who has more power. But no one, not even those who win the political shouting match, will be free.

There resides at the very center of each human life a spiritual dynamism that does not follow the laws of physical motion and is therefore the source of both consciousness and freedom. That center of each human life deserves the name "spirit." We are so familiar with our spiritual being that we easily overlook it or take it for granted. In our everyday life, however, the spiritual is readily at hand with a little self-conscious reflection on what we're doing in human discourse. Suppose we are in conversation with a friend. We grow animated. We draw upon a certain store of physical energy. No matter how enthusiastic one becomes in conversation, one can't keep talking forever. Physical energy is expended; one senses a need to rest, to get some coffee.

But in that conversation, something else is going on as well, even when we are unaware of it. Speaking with precision and attending to the proper character of the conversation is not at all a zero-sum physical transaction, such as when I push a heavy weight or pull a car out of the mud. In these situations, I lose energy because there is a transfer of physical power from me to the object. In exchanging my ideas with others, however, I don't lose them. All of us engage in communication without loss. The scholastic philosophers called this feature of knowing "immanent," an activity that remains in the knower even as it passes into another knower. The wonder is that, while it does remain in the speaker, it also becomes present to and in the friend with whom he or she is speaking, at least to the degree that the speaker has been clear and the friend attentive. This is the first law of the spiritual activity of knowing and communicating. It isn't subject to the laws of thermodynamics. It isn't technological. Human beings have been conversing for a long time. We are social animals or, in more contemporary terms, animals who speak.

There is still more to be gleaned from this very ordinary activity of conversing with another human person. The German philosopher G. W. F. Hegel (1770–1831) pointed out that consciousness has the capability of going out to the other, of identifying with the other and returning to itself, all the while retaining its own identity without loss. In going out to the other and in recognizing it and understanding it, no matter how superficial or partial our knowledge might be, the mind doesn't intrude upon the other. The other remains other. Even as I know the recipe for making pie, the recipe remains a recipe. Knowing as distinct from musing occurs only when we are present to the thing as it really is. Knowing is not reverie; it is attention to the object on the object's own terms. Dreaming about pie won't feed me; I have to know the recipe.

Our wonder is increased if we attend to what is going on in our own person. As I write, I know I have a relationship to the room in which I am writing, and the reader has a similar relationship to his or her room. This relationship is different from the physical relationship by which the chair settles under one's weight or we bump into tables if we're not careful while going for a coffee break. Too easily we think of our knowledge of the room as putting images and ideas in our heads. It's true that we retain residual ideas and images in memory once we've left this room. But in actually knowing the room at the time we're in it, we don't put ideas in our heads as though we were placing pictures in a miniature art gallery. Our actual knowing of the room puts us into the room in a nonphysical way. I'm already in the room physically in my body, and I'm once again in the same room in my being aware of it. I am doubly present in and to the room: in physical existence and in intentional existence. Insofar as we know the objects in this room in some fashion, we do not put them into our heads. On the contrary, we're cast into the room in a new and distinct and wondrous way. For insofar as we know the objects, we don't bump into them or upset tables or press down on chairs in ways that are going to leave us in physical trouble; yet we are truly present to them, not just physically proximate to them.

The wonder of knowing is that it's not governed by the justly famous three laws of physics. Rather, knowing is noninvasive to the thing known, and it comes about in us by our submitting to the way things really are in themselves. The truth of things governs our knowing them, and knowing them invites us and frees us to act. Even painful truth brings a certain enrichment because it enables us to know our situation truly. In the very center of the human person, therefore, at the spiritual source that is governed and perfected by truth, we come upon the secret of human freedom and the bond between freedom and truth. Truth has the power to convince us and to attract us. Truth opens us up

to ourselves, to others, and to our world. Truth is th
draws us out of this deadening passivity into th
genuinely spiritual existence and genuinely personal life, the life
of freedom. That is why freedom cannot be divorced from truth
and why we can't try to divorce them from each other in making the case for personal human dignity. Our dignity as persons
has its roots in the freedom that images God and is brought to
self-consciousness from natural reason and from responding to
God's own gracious self-revelation. This freedom lays upon us the
adventure and responsibility of acting in accordance with the
truth received, including the truth about human nature. Our
moral actions originate in our freedom, by which we corrobo-
rate our nature or are at war against it. Moral actions develop us
as persons; they qualify our life. In that sense, to know the truth
is itself a moral activity and to lie is immoral and diminishes us.

In a materialist schema, which doesn't recognize this spirituality of knowing and the freedom of acting, problems in scientific and technological advances become acute both morally
and in the realm of truth itself. If freedom precedes knowing
and giving and is not intrinsically related to both, there is pure
indetermination or indifference in assessing competing truth
claims, and there is no need to pursue the truth of a situation.
There is need only to affirm oneself in this battle of opinions
and conflicting physical forces, so that one will survive and be
able to make a certain difference in one's life on one's own
terms. It's not a matter, in a materialist philosophy, of discovering oneself through looking for the truth of things and through
generously giving oneself to this truth. It is a matter, rather, of
discovering oneself through a willed self-affirmation that leads
to a disordered desire for control over every aspect of human

life and, therefore, to warring against the human condition itself and to a resentment against it, which are spiritually destructive. Even the Greek myths often illustrate this battle, usually tragically.

This question of the relation between truth and freedom also runs through St. Paul's letters. Paul writes about how truth and freedom are the capacities of a human person who has been set free by God's grace to know the truth about Christ and who can therefore know how to act as a responsible person in the world. "For freedom," St. Paul writes, "Christ has set us free; stand fast therefore and do not submit again to the yoke of slavery" (Gal 5:1). "You were called to freedom, brethren; only do not use your freedom as an opportunity for the flesh; but through love be servants of one another" (Gal 5:13). In St. Paul's Second Letter to the Corinthians, following Christ means sharing in the Spirit given us, possessing and living in freedom. But it's not an immediately perfected life. Spiritual work is to be done. There is growth in freedom. This is not only so in the acquiring of virtue; it's true also, obviously, for human skills like playing the piano. One is not free to make music until, over a long period, one submits oneself to the discipline of learning, starting with scales and going through many hours of practice to master the instrument in order to be truly free in playing it. Such is the case in one's life with the Lord. Freedom is not there in the beginning; there is a submission in which we slowly discover how, in daily offering ourselves to the Lord for his purposes, he truly sets us free.

This understanding of how person, knowledge and freedom, self-consciousness and self-giving, interrelate is at odds with the laws of our country right now. That is extremely unfortunate, because law is the great carrier of American culture. Law is the only thing we all have in common. In a culture and a country where there is no common race, not even a common first language, and there is no totally common culture, it is law that tells us what is right and wrong, and it is law that determines the truth of things. When law gets thoroughly politicized, when judges are subservient to the ideologies of political parties, there is no genuine truth in public discourse, there are only some people with a majority of votes and other people without a majority.

The famous "mystery passage" that the Supreme Court endorsed in determining *Planned Parenthood v. Casey,* the decision that confirmed the constitutional right to an abortion, said that the essence of human personhood or the center of our life as human beings is the ability to control and to define for oneself the meaning and purpose of life. Since government has no place in this determination, and neither do families or churches, one is left to his or her own devices. That passage enshrines in law the sense of freedom as personal autonomy, freedom divorced from all relationships. It is freedom divorced from the truth of things.

Definitions of the human person work themselves out practically in U.S. society in family law and civil laws governing marriage. They work themselves out similarly in the community of faith: in John Paul II's letter on families, *Familiaris consortio* (1981), and in Vatican II's *Gaudium et spes* (1965). They work themselves out in dialogue with those who share our society: with secular humanists open to engaging people of faith on the one hand and with religious fundamentalists on the other.

While noting the possibility for dialogue with secular humanists, I would like to signal especially the new challenge to our understanding of the human person encountered in a resurgent fideism, a kind of fundamentalism found sometimes in the

Catholic Church, which has its own sort of fideism, sometimes in fundamentalist Protestantism, but now especially in some Islamic movements. I mention fundamentalism not in the pejorative sense in which that term is sometimes used to banish these groups politically but in the sense of a classical epistemological fideism, where reason has nothing to contribute to understanding either faith or the human person. In fundamentalist thought, the only legitimate access to truth is from a religious authority, and there can be no shared rational insight about a common human nature. In the Church's tradition, this is a seriously truncated approach to human intelligence, to Catholic faith, and to the common good.

Finally, we are analyzing what it means to be human from several perspectives (from a materialist view caught up in technological advance; from the light of faith that is given us along with human reflection; from a fundamentalist reading of the human person) in order to construct a culture of life. How does one create a culture of life, how is culture to be transformed, when there are such divergent understandings of the human person? In *Evangelium vitae* (1995), Pope John Paul II set out five steps necessary to create a culture of life, and we can take these steps while striving to understand where others are coming from and in dialogue with them. Only then can Catholics hope to find the allies who will help us build a culture of life. Even if we don't completely share convictions about human personhood, we can work together for certain limited goals.

The first step in creating a culture of life is to form consciences that recognize the incomparable and inviolable worth of every human life and appreciate the essential connection between human life and freedom. No one wants to be a "routinized person," sunk in tedium and believing that nothing can ever change. That's not why life is given us, and, in the quest for the bases of human dignity and human freedom, we'll find many allies among other Christians and other believers and also some secular humanists who are concerned about human freedom and respect for human life.

Second, to create a culture of life one has to recover the necessary link between human freedom and truth. Allies are harder to find in achieving this goal. For some, truth is one thing and it tells us how to manipulate things; or, if you want to get beyond that, it tells us how things really are. But truth doesn't tell us how we ourselves really are because we establish ourselves freely only when we act according to our own purpose or desires. The essential connection between our understanding of who we truly are and our ability to give ourselves to what is good can't be made outside of a culture open to and protective of all human life.

Third, education about human sexuality is necessary for creating a culture of life. Education that respects human personhood will foster respect for life and promote a deeper understanding of human sexuality and responsible procreation, of suffering and death in human experience. Here Catholics find many allies among evangelical Protestants.

Fourth, to create a culture of life we have to adopt a new lifestyle, one that places primacy on the importance of being over having, of persons over things. While they wouldn't use that vocabulary, we might find many allies in achieving this goal among those in the ecological movement. With those who truly appreciate the wonder of nature, one can raise the question about nature giving us norms on its terms rather than ours.

Last, in order to see the world as it is, Catholics have to foster a contemplative outlook. Here, again, sometimes there are human allies, but the final ally is God himself. The world reveals itself to the silent listener and only to him or her. The more silently one listens, the more purely one is able to perceive reality. Pope Paul VI preached in a homily for the Feast of the Holy Family in 1964: "[W]e learn from silence. If only we could once again appreciate its great value. We need this wonderful state of mind, beset as we are by the cacophony of strident protests and conflicting claims so characteristic of these turbulent times. The silence of Nazareth should teach us how to meditate in peace and quiet, to reflect on the deeply spiritual and to be open to the voice of God's inner wisdom and the counsel of his true teachers. Nazareth can teach us the value of study and preparation, of meditation, of a well-ordered personal spiritual life, and of silent prayer that is known only to God." In a God who acts for the good of his human creatures, a God who wants us to know and love him, we have the final guarantor of our freedom.

5

THE HUMAN BODY
AND PERSONAL FREEDOM:
MADE IN GOD'S IMAGE AND LIKENESS*

Pope Paul VI, when he visited the United Nations in New York in 1965, said that the Church is an "expert in humanity." This was not a personal boast but a historical claim. Having accompanied the human journey for two thousand years, the Church possesses a wisdom that is grounded both in God's self-revelation and also in the experience of having lived through diverse historic events of great significance in understanding the human condition. The Church's conversation is first of all with God, but it is, even in that conversation, broader than the question of individual salvation. Human beings are social beings, and our salvation is social as well. The Church herself is a public institution and must be concerned not just for the individual but for the common good, which she speaks to in her social and ethical teaching. The common good of human beings addresses bodily needs as well as spiritual concerns. Understanding ourselves as embodied

*This chapter was originally presented as "Christian Vision for Moral Decisions of Bioethics," an address given at the seventh annual conference of The Center for Bioethics & Human Dignity in Deerfield, Illinois, on July 21, 2000 (http://cbhd.org/node/403).

spirits brings a distinctive light to the public conversation on advances in biology and related sciences.

The conversation shaping public policy on bioethics has both a scientific and a social base. First, we need to examine the framework that is the scientific base and ask whether it is adequate to the reality discussed; and second, we need to look at the political and legal framework that is the social base for the public conversation that establishes public policy governing bioethics. The two frameworks cannot be entirely separated, especially in decisions about public policy. The greatest challenge to an adequate conversation is a reductionism that distorts the full reality of the human subject.

Because all human beings are embodied, the United Nations has created a global forum on ethics and biology. Article I of the Universal Declaration on the Human Genome and Human Rights, which was adopted unanimously by the members of UNESCO in 1997, states: "The human genome underlies the fundamental unity of all members of the human family, as well as the recognition of their inherent dignity and diversity. In a symbolic sense, it is the heritage of humanity." The document goes on to urge the governments of the world to foster research on the human genome so that all people may take advantage of scientific progress based on it.

Such research, according to the declaration, should be directed toward alleviating human suffering and improving health, while research that is "contrary to human dignity" or the human rights of individuals should be avoided. But these rights are not further defined, and, without such further clarification, the danger of reductionism inevitably arises. The Holy See, as an official observer to the UN, pointed out some of the shortcomings of Article I during the drafting sessions. It objected to the use of terms that seemed to reduce the common ground of humanity to a simple biological basis, as if our personhood is a function of our brains and our dignity is based upon our genetic code. The Holy See also argued that the UN formulation did not sufficiently emphasize the need to protect each human being from the moment of conception, when each human being receives his or her individual genetic identity from his or her parents.

Critics of the declaration, and of Article I in particular, have pointed out that the emphasis on common heritage in order to protect the human genome runs the risk of robbing individuals of their identity, especially if it implies only a biological basis for our common humanity. This view risks creating a society in which any person who lacks genetic perfection or has a variation from the norm could be judged to fall outside the boundaries of our common humanity. The declaration does not include in the public conversation society's obligation to respect human dignity at every stage of life. While it explicitly states that reproductive cloning is to be excluded as a violation of human dignity, it omits offering criteria to determine what other practices might violate individual dignity.

This omission is glaring, given the document's silence about the embryo and fetus. Since the declaration states that one of the goals to be advanced by all nations is prevention of genetically based and genetically influenced diseases, it could be read to oblige or at least encourage nation-states to engage in eugenic practices such as genetic abortions or preimplantation genetic selection of acceptable embryos. Even racist forms of eugenics

are not ruled out by the UNESCO declaration. Already there
are reports of families using gender selection as a justification for
abortion or as a criterion for selecting which embryos will be implanted and which discarded. Germ line genetic manipulation
and enhancements of the genome could also arguably fall within
the obligations asserted in the declaration. There's nothing in
the document to suggest that such practices are not in keeping
with human dignity, particularly given the ambiguity of the
suggestion that human dignity is founded upon the genome and
that everyone has a right to take advantage of scientific advances
made through genomic research.

For those lucky enough to be brought to term, the UNESCO
declaration leaves open the possibility of genetic profiling and
the subsequent denial of rights to health care and jobs. It is easy to
imagine that, in such an ambiguous cultural climate, the specters
of assisted suicide and euthanasia would threaten those showing
the first signs of genetic diseases that are otherwise temporary,
treatable, or manageable. Finally, in such a climate, it is not in-
conceivable that even those who are sick or disabled by patho-
gens or accident will be seen as genetically responsible for their
conditions and thus be considered unnecessary social burdens,
to be marginalized and eliminated. Many of the present schemes
for extending universal health care by rationing coverage of some
diseases threaten to leave large numbers of disabled persons more
vulnerable than ever and are resented and feared by them and
their caregivers.

Gradually, perhaps, the need to abort and euthanize "genetically challenged undesirables" may diminish because of our increasing ability to create human beings not just free from disease
but also in possession of characteristics that are indisputably

good: beauty, intelligence, affability, longevity. Initially, the means to these ends will be gamete profiling and selection followed by artificial conception. Eventually, however, even these artificial means of conception might be bypassed through germ cell interventions aimed at tailor-making sperm and eggs.

Finally, the issue of nontherapeutic genetic manipulation now looms before us. This conversation is about positive eugenics accomplished not through coercion but through free choices made possible by a free market in genetic materials. Also imaginable are coerced therapeutic manipulations aimed at limiting the social costs of disease. Putting aside unintended consequences, such as impairment or death, or the intentional production of a useful lower class of human beings, public pressure could build to maximize a host of traits that are indisputably good.

In light of such threats and some existing practices, the public conversation shaping social policy on these matters requires a concrete outline of a systematic understanding of the human person as a subject, a public philosophy that can account for the dignity and inherent value of every human individual at every stage of life. Universally accepted guidelines that give the fullest possible treatment of human dignity, with an explanation of its foundation and its full ethical implications, can then be used to direct biomedical advances along a course that has as its center respect for each human person. When science is guided by such an understanding, it will enhance and promote our dignity instead of creating threats to human life. Without such guidelines, achieving public consensus on how to act and legislate responsibly on life issues remains an intractable problem. Might Church teaching help to preserve human freedom and protect human dignity?

In 1974, years before the UNESCO declaration, the Holy See's Congregation for the Doctrine of the Faith published a declaration on procured abortion and discerned the need to set forth a fuller definition of what it means to be human in response to practices that implicitly deny the humanity of the unborn. It asserted that everyone can know through reason what a human person is and, therefore, come to know society's collective obligations to individual men and women. The document from the congregation says,

> Constituted by a rational nature, man is a personal subject capable of reflecting on himself and of determining his acts and hence his own destiny: he is free. He is consequently master of himself; or rather, because this takes place in the course of time, he has the means of becoming so: this is his task. Created immediately by God, man's soul is spiritual and therefore immortal. Hence man is open to God, he finds his fulfillment only in Him. But man lives in the community of his equals; he is nourished by interpersonal communication with men in the indispensable social setting. In the face of society and other men, each human person possesses himself, he possesses life and different goods, he has these as a right. It is this that strict justice demands from all in this regard.

These were really only the first steps in coming to terms with the challenges posed by biological reductionism. Central to the vision asserted in the 1974 Roman Curia document is the note that what is genetically human is always a personal subject. This aspect often seems to go without notice, even in conversations about human personality when, especially in the UNESCO declaration, man, in the generic sense, is being examined. Beyond the fact that man is an object in a field of objects, man is also a subject. He is not a "what" but a "who." To exclude the subject as part of the assessment of what is meant by inherent human dignity is to miss the basis of that dignity. The UNESCO declaration clearly makes this error when it conceives the unity of humanity to be founded only upon the human genome. On the contrary, the real basis of our unity is our common life as persons in relationship. Even in conversations in the Church, that note has not always been consistently sounded, but the conversation has led to the development of verbal tools that are ever more adequate in addressing the subject.

Pope Leo XIII, at the end of the nineteenth century, argued that freedom can be neither granted nor withheld by the state because it belongs to the human person. In his words, "Man precedes the State, and possesses, prior to the formation of any State, the right of providing for the substance of his body." This understanding puts forth a notion of the state built on social systems natural to human persons, especially the family. This method transcends the ideological framework then being imposed by emerging totalitarian states. The Pope identified structures that meet the person's life-sustaining needs—marriage, family, local communities, work associations, and, finally, society and the state itself. These structures fulfill the person and are necessary to the person's inherent quest for identity.

Leo XIII apprehended that specific works create and sustain human persons; human activities reveal the person. By participation in moments of self-transcendence, the person acquires specific fulfillment and identity. The moments of transcendence include the person's relation to his or her body, which is not an object superadded to a person. Rather, the body is inseparable from the person's humanity. Persons transcend themselves in the everyday moments of life and work; and bodily life and work bear the impress of one's personality. Through life in their family, children continue their parents' personalities and become part of the human heritage. Leo XIII's guidance for creating societies open to transcendence was publicly rejected in this country and elsewhere; and throughout the twentieth century, human history was marked by a series of totalitarian experiments that left the human race severely weakened, in body and spirit.

If the conversation about human dignity begins not with the human genome but with the fuller understanding of personhood presented by the Church, what shape will it take? There are three points to take into consideration when answering this question. First, one will speak of human dignity as a property of human nature received at the moment one comes into existence, something that can be neither gained nor lost throughout the course of one's life. It's given. Second, human dignity will also be understood in terms of an identity achieved, for example, as a wife, a father, a servant of the poor. Existential dignity is intrinsic, but it can be either enhanced or diminished by the kind of life one leads. We are not fully the beings we are meant to be at the moment we come into existence; rather, God grants us the freedom and ability to choose in part what we become. This is the stuff of tragedy when promises are not fulfilled and of triumph when capacities flourish. Third is the dignity that comes to us through freely accepting God's graciously offered gift of salvation and life in him. We are the kinds of beings who can accept God's grace and live as adopted sons and daughters of God. The end of this life of grace is eternal life marked by the fullness of truth and love. We have human dignity in that we are beings who possess the capacity to receive the gift of salvation. This is our destiny, and in the beatific vision we shall be like him, for we shall see him as he is.

These three bases for human dignity are interrelated in all Catholic reflection on the body and human dignity, but they can be explored separately for the sake of public conversation in a pluralistic society. Thus, the ultimate end of human life underlies and directs the first two bases, but it is not usually part of public discourse in our country. We should, however, have the right in a free society to acknowledge it and to invoke it, even knowing that it cannot be universally persuasive in a pluralistic society.

The second aspect, that of existential or achieved human dignity, is more accessible to human reason without the aid of God's self-revelation and therefore provides an appropriate beginning for a broader discussion of public policy.

More problematic in the public discussion of human dignity is the first claim that it is endowed, given in its origins, and therefore carried by each genetically distinct individual as a member of the human species, no matter the stage of development. It takes some work to "see" a human person in an embryo. It's methodologically easier therefore to work back from the already emergent "I," the subject. If the self is only a center of action, the self disappears when action is not possible. But if the self is a continuum, the subjective underpinning for action or potential action at any moment of development, it remains a subject of inviolable dignity in all circumstances.

One way into the discussion is to pose the question: At what point did you become a person? Every time a child is born, we acknowledge the existence of the self without great evidence. We declare the infant to be a person, at least in this stage in the development of our legal system, even though it does not exhibit the rationality or volitional behavior that we associate with the actions of a human person. What we mean is that this young one is an emergent "I" with a subjectivity distinct from but like our own. We instinctively ascribe personhood to the child since it is through the prism of person that the subject "I" will emerge. We believe this and we know it from experience, even when there are problems in the full emergence of a subject able to think and to will and to walk.

Some elements in the story of one's coming into possession of oneself can be remembered and referred to in questions that create a public conversation. Can you remember when you began to tell time? Can you remember when you were first able to tie your shoelaces? Can you remember when you could first read a map for your father driving the car? Can you remember moments of religious conversion, when God became present in an extraordinary way? These are questions that bring to full consciousness elements in the development of personal subjectivity that become part of the public conversation when we lament the death of a child, when a beloved human person is cut off at a moment that was obviously tragic. These are moments that lead us to an appreciation of personal continuity throughout a lifetime of action and achievement.

From our own experience, then, we can begin to appreciate why it is morally wrong to freeze a human embryo. In doing so, we take it upon ourselves to halt the dynamic, natural process of development and hold this person's expression of his or her own selfhood captive. Just as no one would be justified in preventing a child from coming to adolescence through hormone injections, so it is wrong to deprive even the embryo of his or her development and growth. In God's eyes, and in our beliefs, it doesn't matter if you're ten seconds old following initial conception or a hundred years old waiting to die. Life is life, and persons are persons.

Further harm is done to human dignity when an embryo is destroyed and its stem cells removed for research or therapies. These cells would have become the material structures allowing personal human expression, but they are instead artificially directed to develop into various forms of tissues to treat the diseases of others. Instead of a unique subjective self in all its dimensions, what emerges is a medical commodity. This redirection hijacks the embryo's powers of cell division, specialization, and growth, and bends them to another's will. Though the goal of alleviating human suffering is praiseworthy, the means violate the God-given rights of the embryo and ignore the image and likeness of God found in every human person.

Why is it so difficult to "see" a human person from the moment of conception? A human person as such can't be quantified and therefore can't be known through the usual methods of physical science. Yet even within the terms of the scientific method itself, there are conclusions for which there is no direct proof. The thesis of dark matter filling the universe is a case of inferring the existence of something that cannot be seen. For years, mathematicians, cosmologists, and physicists predicted the discovery of black holes. Gravity so overwhelms space and time as to compress it into what is no longer discernible empirically, a singularity in cosmology. We can see through the Hubble

Telescope event horizons in which star masses seem to be consumed or energy released, yet the black holes themselves are never seen. Scientists have theorized that a black hole is situated in the center of every galactic spiral, and its size can be predicted from the speed of the stars in the outermost arm of that galaxy. This prediction explains the formation of star systems into galactic clusters, but it is observed only in what we have come to consider its effects. The evidence is not directly observable, but it is persuasive because it is consonant with and necessary to understand what is perceived.

Analogously, we infer personhood from the evidence of its effects. For example, the most powerful human intuitions are born of love. In a marriage based on mutual love and respect, a wife knows how her husband will act and can predict what he will do from past experience. This is the kind of evidence that surrounds the Resurrection narratives in the Gospels. Peter and John run to the tomb together. Peter is puzzled. John looks at the empty tomb and the folded cloths and, through an intuition born of love, knows that Christ is risen. John is the "beloved disciple." Here is the center of human subjectivity, a term and a reality that have to be part of an adequate public discussion on bioethics and on the morality of various scientific procedures.

Closely related to subjectivity is the term "individual rights." Its invocation moves the discussion from an anthropological and scientific universe into a political and legal one. We are more used to talking publicly about human rights than about the biological bases for human dignity. The U.S. Constitution contains a Bill of Rights, but only since the UN Universal Declaration of the Rights of Man has the word "rights" taken center stage in global ethical discourse. In our legal system, rights are prima facie warrants for individual freedom at several levels, so long as they do not overstep the rights of others. This philosophy of rights is agnostic about all human values except freedom, since the safeguarding of individual freedom is sufficient to assure the preservation of all other values. Unfortunately, without a connection to truth, freedom can be arbitrary, depending solely on the desires of the individual citizen. What can come to predominate in establishing human value is the structure of pleasure or pain in the marketplace of emotions.

The corrective to this deficient understanding of human rights is found in Pope John XXIII's *Pacem in terris* (1963). In this encyclical, for the first time in the two hundred years since the French Revolution, the Church used the language of human rights in an official document. The term had been used before in the Salamanca School of legal jurisprudence, after the Spaniards came in contact with the indigenous peoples of this hemisphere and came to recognize them as human beings with rights. But because of the French Revolution, the Church abandoned this language, so terrible had been its use in justifying the persecution of the Church and the slaughter of priests and nuns. Only very gingerly did the Church come back to a language that is modern but does reflect a basic dimension of human dignity.

In *Pacem in terris,* John XXIII set out a system of rights with the individual person at the center of a series of concentric interpersonal circles that define the complexities of human endeavor. Rights are understood to be both natural and personal. They define social structures necessary to human integrity; and the presumption behind this understanding is that the human individual is a person. As a rational being, the person is therefore first and foremost a moral enterprise, and moral relations define the rights of individual persons. More particularly, they clarify what is needed to safeguard personal integrity, so that what offends personal integrity in any manner offends human dignity and should not be legally recognized as a right.

In *Pacem in terris,* John XXIII wrote: "The same law of nature that governs the life and conduct of individuals must also regulate the relations of political communities. . . . Political leaders . . . are still bound by the natural law . . . and they have no authority to depart from its slightest precepts." Introducing natural law into the public debate signals a departure from the social contract understandings of eighteenth-century political theory; it is a clearly different voice and not much respected in cultures built upon choice. In *Veritatis splendor,* Pope John Paul II wrote, "When it is a matter of the moral norms prohibiting intrinsic evil, there are no privileges or exceptions for anyone." He added, "It makes no difference whether one is the master of the world or the 'poorest of the poor' on the face of the earth. Before the demands of morality, we are all absolutely equal." What protects democracy and the public conversation that supports it is not a sense of freedom that pits every man against the others but the conviction that every human being is intrinsically equal to every other. To quote *Veritatis splendor* once more: These exceptionless negative moral norms "in fact represent the unshakable foundation and solid guarantee of a just and peaceful human coexistence, and hence of genuine democracy, which can come into being and develop only on the basis of the equality of all its members, who possess common rights and duties."

I am not sanguine that the public conversation about bioethical policy will be sufficiently morally informed and anthropologically sound to protect both individuals and their inherent human dignity and society itself from becoming an example of Aldous Huxley's fictitious *Brave New World*. The paradigm of popular public discourse in this country is usually an individual's dream, the American dream, thwarted by reactionary authoritarian oppressors, particularly religious oppressors. Universities as guardians of reasoned discourse are also subject to many influences other than the purely rational. On questions of bioethical policy, sources of funding for medical and pharmaceutical research often play a role. The bishops have lost much of their moral authority and therefore speak without great influence. The courts have played an ambiguous role by explaining that they're making moral arguments by placing themselves above morality. It is a strange argument to decide what is just based on the fact that you are ignoring theories of what is right and what is wrong.

With or without adequate foundations for public discussion and decision making, steady scientific progress in discovering the biological bases of human life goes on. The announcement that the federal government's Human Genome Project had succeeded—ahead of schedule—in mapping the nucleotide sequences of all twenty-three pairs of chromosomes belonging to five human persons places humanity at the threshold of the Enlightenment project's final frontier. At the core of this modern project, a project not unrelated in its genesis to Christian values, is the notion of the intrinsic value of each human person and the subsequent desire to liberate all persons from the limitations that physical nature imposes on the human body. According to the merely secular version of modernity, the means to this freedom and fulfillment for all are the free economy, the liberal democratic state, and, above all, the scientific method of sensory observation and inductive logic that reveals the material and efficient causes at work in both physical and human affairs. Truly marvelous scientific progress makes it clear that the final frontier is the human body itself. In Pope John Paul II's words, "The human genome in a way is the last continent to be explored."[1]

While personally anxious about the possibility of adequate public discourse in this realm, as a believer I am hopeful that the third dimension of human dignity mentioned above, our graced reality, might be attractive enough to influence public decision making in bioethics. What does the Word made flesh tell us about the human body and human dignity? The risen Christ is not constrained by the laws of physical nature; his is a body that is incorruptible. He is completely free. Like us, Jesus is a human being, born of a human mother, the Virgin Mary. From Mary's womb he emerged a man, like us in all things but sin, with a human physical body. From his tomb after the Crucifixion also emerged a man, but no longer entirely like us in his body. For, having passed through a fully human life and having overcome the ultimate barrier, death itself, he emerged transformed, possessing what St. Paul calls a "spiritual body," truly his, and still physical, but transformed in ways that Scripture does not detail.

In his First Letter to the Corinthians (15:36–44), St. Paul says that God provides each living thing—plants, animals, humans, and even the heavenly bodies—with the kind of body appropriate to it. Even death does not prevent this embodiment. The apparently dead seed in the ground rises in a new, leafy, and fruitful body. Paul applies this insight to the human body resurrected from the dead: "What is sown is perishable, what is raised is imperishable. It is sown in dishonor, it is raised in glory. It is sown in weakness, it is raised in power. It is sown a physical body, it is raised a spiritual body" (Cor 15:42–44).

There is a technical distinction in Paul's vocabulary between natural and resurrected bodies. He describes the body both as *sarx,* which is the element of limitation and corruption in our bodies, the result of sin, and as *soma,* a more neutral term that indicates a body capable of being transformed spiritually while remaining truly material. The body's principle of life in our time and space is *psyche,* or soul. Its principle of life in its risen state is *spirit.* The risen Christ has become a life-giving spirit, Paul says, in whose likeness believers will be raised. Limitation and corruption cannot inherit the Kingdom of God, and, at the Last Judgment, *sarx* is destroyed and *soma* becomes incorruptible and immortal. The nature of "spiritual bodies," other than the certitude that they are human bodies transformed, is not revealed. In the vocabulary of Scripture and in the experience of visionaries whose holiness seems authentic, light is the metaphor that comes closest to grasping this transformation. Modern studies of light as energy give those who want to use physical science to pursue this question of supernatural faith in bodily resurrection an important opening, it seems to me, for responsible speculation.

If, according to Christian faith, Jesus is the firstborn from the dead, the first of the human race to have passed in his body through the limitations of matter, then it is the history of his body that tells us the meaning, nature, and destiny of our bodies. The body is integral to salvation history because Jesus our Savior, in his own flesh, has risen from the dead. An origin in time shows that salvation is not an escape into eternity. The bridge between *psyche,* or the soul as natural, and spirit, the soul as immortal, clothed with divine glory by the power of the Holy Spirit of God, is the transformation that evangelists and doctrinal theologians call "resurrection from the dead." Just as natural life is a gift, so is risen life pure gift. But between the one and the other comes the crucifixion of the body—Jesus' act of total self-sacrifice made possible, in part, by his material human body. In the light of faith, the gift of this life must be surrendered, willingly sacrificed, so that the gift of eternal life can be received.

In light of the paradox involving the incontestable superiority of the resurrected and unconstrained body, a distinctively Christian bioethical vision can be formulated. A Christian bioethical vision is grounded in the truths about the human person that revelation discloses in the body of the risen Christ. First among these is the dignity or value of each human person at every stage and condition of life. Even without the aid of revelation, the uniqueness of each human being, along with the implications of natural law precepts and, most tellingly of all, the intentional affective response to persons that is commonly called "love," would recommend this truth to us. But additionally, the revelation of our likeness to and relationship with God, especially as revealed through the Incarnation of Christ and his self-sacrifice, incontestably attests to this truth. The God in whose image we are created knows and consecrates each of us in the womb, and he sent his only begotten Son, his Eternal Word, to become flesh and die for us on the Cross. In this light, acts that manipulate, marginalize, or kill innocent human persons in any phase or condition are grave offenses that should be proscribed even by civil law.

Finally, the Christian vision sees not only the intrinsic value of persons but also their true fulfillment. Our creation in God's image underlies the conviction that we are fulfilled by freely giving ourselves to others. While our capacities to reason and choose are evidence of our being made in the image of God, these capacities ultimately exist in service of our social or transcendent nature, our common vocation to freely share our gifts for the good of others. The relationship between freedom and fulfillment becomes clear in light of God's self-revelation in Christ. Free human acts not only reveal the nature of the self to itself; they also constitute the person, who thus cocreates himself or herself in a limited but real sense. Persons are never autonomous, but they are self-directed. Assisted by grace as a principle of action, we become ourselves by freely giving ourselves to what is most valuable and capable of loving in return, to other human persons and to God. Conversely, we thwart our destiny when we refuse to enter into self-giving and self-sacrificing relationships oriented toward the good and the life of others. In contravening the dignity of others, we arrest our own human fulfillment. Human perfection, if it is not a gift from God, is a self-destructive ideal.

The human person who is created for communion with others is a unity of soul and body. In his catechetical reflections on human sexuality, Pope John Paul II reminded us that Aquinas's thinking on the doctrine of the resurrection of the body led to his definitive move away from a Platonic characterization of the real person as the immaterial soul, with the body as only a problematic prison. As better described by Aristotle, the soul is the animating or unifying principle or "form" of the body. The person is a unity composed of a soul that expresses itself through and is conditioned by its body.

In this vision of the person, the human body, including its sense faculties, from which all knowledge of even moral truths begins, and its limitations, is essential to the development and salvation of the whole person. God-given and natural bodily functioning, including sexual activity, is morally significant because it promotes the perfection of the whole person. John Paul II's personalistic reading of the natural law tradition argues that ethical principles derived by natural law from reflection on bodily finalities are not guilty of physicalism, naturalism, or biologism: Functions of human nature and the body "constitute a reference point for moral decisions" and provide "rational indications with regard to the order of morality. . . . Indeed, natural inclinations take on moral relevance only insofar as they refer to the human person and his authentic fulfillment. . . . The person, by the light of reason and the support of virtue, discovers in the body the anticipatory signs, the expression and promise of the gift of self, in conformity with the wise plan of the Creator" (*Veritatis splendor* 48).

In other words, both Christian revelation and reason tell us that the normally functioning body that God provides for us is good because it promotes the perfection and the salvation of the whole person. The body, with its need for development and its limitations that temper our strength, intelligence, personality, and longevity, is integral to the development of virtues such as humility and generosity, which allow us to give ourselves to others. Following St. Paul's cue, we also "rejoice in our weakness," our "treasure in earthen vessels," because it puts us clearly in need of God, thus drawing us closer to the ultimate source of our fulfillment. Additionally, the complementarity of these limitations constitutes the many gifts that draw us closer to one another. What the Pope says in *Salvifici doloris* (1984, 30) about the meaning of suffering also pertains to other limitations. Like the pain of disease, all natural bodily limitations are "present in the world in order to release love, in order to give birth to works of love toward neighbor, in order to transform the whole of human civilization into a 'civilization of love.'"

What of attempts to create a new humanity, beyond our present limits, but to do so on our own, without receiving new life as a gift from God? The qualities that nontherapeutic genetic enhancements would seek to obtain can be good, and the motives for pursuing them may also be good. But one can imagine so-called superhumans who, less burdened by limitations, struggles, and the need for God and others, become self-centered and isolated, and thus less than fully human. The best human life in this world is therefore not one freed from all physical constraints. One could imagine this self-centeredness being directed against those who, lacking access to gene-enhancing technology, might find themselves part of a grossly disadvantaged and permanently objectified underclass. Even those not directly benefiting from such enhancements would find themselves in danger of seeing persons as products to be created according to individual desires and needs. The public conversation would then ignore the openness toward all that is the core of an authentic humanism.

A poem titled "Letter to Genetically Engineered Super Humans" by a young writer named Fred Dings nicely sums up many of these intuitions about genetic engineering when it is used to contravene the vision of the human body as a gift.

You are the children of our fantasies of form,
our wish to carve a larger cave of light,
our dream to perfect the ladder of genes and climb

its rungs to the height of human possibility,
to a stellar efflorescence beyond all injury
and disease, with minds as bright as newborn suns

and bodies which leave our breathless mirrors stunned.
Forgive us if we failed to imagine your loneliness
in the midst of all that ordinary excellence,

if we failed to understand how much harder
it would be to build the bridge of love
between such splendid selves, to find the path

of humility among the labyrinth of your abilities,
to be refreshed without forgetfulness,
and weave community without the threads of need.

Forgive us if you must re-invent our flaws
because we failed to guess the simple fact
that the best lives must be less than perfect.[2]

A Christian and adequately human vision of the future of
bioethical research requires planning how to bring new concerns
to culture, including the culture of universities and scientific
communities. Because major elements of our life together are
now regularly submitted for decision to the courts, our society's
treatment of bioethical issues will inevitably be shaped by legal

constraints and the decisions of judges and lawyers regarding embryo experimentation and storage, cloning, artificial conception procedures, prenatal diagnoses, abortion, genetic profiling, assisted suicide, euthanasia, and nontherapeutic genetic engineering. It is, therefore, more urgent than ever to work together to foster a vision of bioethics open to what God tells us about ourselves and to consider carefully how to best translate that vision and the principles derived from it into our culture, our system of law, and the public conversation it sustains.

6

God and Warfare:
Defending Yourself While
Forgiving Your Enemies

Since peace is a sign of God's presence, how can believers in God justifiably go to war? Are there activities that cannot speak of God, that make it impossible to cooperate with him? Warfare is a case that seems intractable because it involves killing neighbors loved by God.

The Second Vatican Council's *Pastoral Constitution on the Church in the Modern World* (*Gaudium et spes*, 1965) spoke of peace as an eschatological reality that will be realized and seen for what it is only when "Christ hands over to the Father a kingdom, eternal and universal, a kingdom of truth and life, of holiness and grace, of justice, love and peace." But before that final moment, that peaceful kingdom begins to be present now, particularly in the mystery of the Church. The Church is the efficacious sign of Christ's reign. The Kingdom of God will not come without the mission and the ministry of the Church, which works to sanctify the world and to make it a more just and peaceful place from generation to generation. The Church is the protagonist and servant of Christ's peace.

The peace described in Church documents is not just any kind of peace, nor is it peace at any price. It's a gift from God. By the power of the Holy Spirit, every believer in Christ searches for peace first of all within his or her own soul, harmonizing always the faith we have received from the apostles with our own behavior, our own desires, our own way. Out of the courage that comes from living that struggle for internal peace, we should find ourselves peacemakers, able to foster peace both in our interpersonal relationships and in building up the new covenant community of the Church, so that God might use the Church as an agent for peace in the world. It is particularly the baptized and confirmed lay faithful, having the common good in view and acting in conformity with the Gospel and the teaching of the Church, who shape temporal realities with Christian commitment, by which the baptized show that they are witnesses and agents of Christ's Kingdom of justice and peace.

St. Augustine called the peace that begins on earth "the tranquillity of order."[1] It is not an order that is merely personal; it is social. It is the ordered fruit of justice; but justice in Scripture means right relationships, not abstract equality. It means that everything is in order, everything is related, everyone is related as God wants them to be. This tranquillity of order is always imperfect in our own souls and also in our community and among nations unless it is complemented by forgiveness. Forgiveness doesn't overlook the need to right the wrong done, but neither does it demand that an enemy forgive you before you will forgive him or her. Forgiveness is given freely, even to someone who doesn't deserve it, because our forgiveness of one another is based on the fulfillment that characterizes the Kingdom of God, who forgives us even when we are sinners. The social teaching of the Church, drawn from the Gospel, insists that the pillars of true peace, therefore, are justice or right order and that form of love that is forgiveness. These ways of acting reconcile those whose peace, whose right order has been unjustly undermined with those guilty of injuring them, or rupturing their peace.

War undermines or even destroys the tranquillity of order. St. Gregory of Nyssa said in the fourth century, "When the civil war in our own nature has been brought to an end and we are at peace within ourselves, then we may become peace for others, agents of that peace which is a gift from God and a sign of Christ's kingdom."[2] That struggle goes on as long as we are fallen creatures living in a fallen world. Constant effort is necessary if the gift of peace is not to slip from our grasp, because the effects of original sin, of personal sin, and of social sin are everywhere in evidence. A utopian vision that doesn't take into account the fallenness of our nature and of the world is just whistling in the dark. The Church, which is very realistic, has tried to come to an understanding of who we are as men and women destined for God's eternal kingdom of peace but living now in our own sinfulness and in sinful social structures. Consequently, the Church has tried to apply a moral vision not only to the search for peace but also to the conduct of war.

In our fallen world, a nation's recourse to military force can be a necessity. The Church honors peacemakers and holds them up for veneration. At the same time, being always faithful to

Jesus Christ and to the work of justice and charity to which he calls his followers, a country may find it necessary to use force in some fashion. St. Augustine, in the fifth century, took this into account in developing just war theory. According to the Catechism of the Catholic Church, "Peace cannot be obtained on earth without safeguarding the goods of persons, free communication among men and women, respect for the dignity of all persons and of all peoples, and the assiduous practice of fraternity."[3] The point here is simply that, in the actual human situation, our duty of love toward our neighbor and our responsibility for those in our care can oblige the use of force. The teaching of the Church, therefore, addresses the possibility of a just war, the use of force in immediate self-defense at least, and perhaps in other ways, provided certain conditions are fulfilled.

Just war theory is the outcome of both our own conviction as disciples of Christ and a philosophical analysis of the moral condition of the human race. In its intent and purpose, just war theory expresses the will for peace. It includes an abhorrence of war even while it recognizes that, in a given situation, it may be necessary for a state to use force to protect the rights of its own people, particularly of its innocent citizens. Just war theory in traditional Catholic social teaching offers principles for defending oneself or defending those for whom one is responsible in a way that is morally justifiable.

In formulating his theory, St. Augustine looked at war as both the result of sin and a remedy for sin in the life of political societies as they actually exist. In certain controlled cases, war could be used by a state that has the duty of holding back an enemy who would injure its people. Therefore, the most potent justification for war for those seeking to act always in union with God is to protect the innocent from certain harm. If there is compelling evidence that harm will come to noncombatants and that this harm is grave and substantial, then the very love of neighbor to which we are enjoined as disciples of Christ may require resort to force. The potential harm might be directed at one's own civilians or it might involve combatants of another country. It is necessary to put one's own combatants in danger rather than to stand by as the innocent are slaughtered. This understanding is the basis not only for defending one's own country but also for intervening in another country.

Pope Benedict XVI, speaking at the United Nations in 2008, emphasized the duty of both individual states and the international community to protect innocent lives, always by peaceful negotiation or the pressure of protest and the exercise of politics first: "The principle of 'responsibility to protect' was considered by the ancient law of nations as the foundation of every action taken by those in government with regard to the governed."[4] The classical principles of just war were formulated in the conditions of warfare in the first Christian millennium and then adjusted with the development of modern nation-states. These principles have evolved in response to changed political institutions and different methods of waging war. Yet the basic theory remains, with its considerations on the legitimate use of armed force and its description of how morally legitimate war must be conducted.

Just war theory is not simply a moral theory in the Church. It has an impact even on the policies and strategies of countries. It wasn't much spoken about in the United States during the Second World War, when the cause for war was unquestionably response to invasion. There was a clear right to go to war, a *jus ad bellum*. But just war theory was very much spoken about at the time of the Vietnam War, at the time of the first Gulf War, and before the invasion of Iraq. In the middle of the twentieth century the Second World War had become a total war. It was people against people, and the distinction between combatant and noncombatant, which is essential to arguments about the moral use of force, was ignored. Some claimed that, in total war, every citizen is a combatant. This attitude led to the firebombing of whole cities and the use of atomic weapons. In 1945, the United States used means to end the war that are clearly immoral in just war theory because they do not respect the distinction between combatant and noncombatant. The *jus in bello*, the constraint to conduct war in a moral way, had to be rethought with the stockpiling of nuclear weapons. Just war theory struggled to adjust to changing circumstances.

Since every government has a right and obligation to defend its people, there was a *jus ad bellum* after the events of September 11, 2001, when our country was attacked not by another country but by a terrorist movement. This situation created a conflict outside the rules for classical just war theory. Once a country is engaged in a war against terrorism, what are the conditions necessary to morally judge the conduct of that war? What are the moral limitations on our response? What is the context in which we have to decide what further action is warranted, even if the war itself remains justified?

The Catholic Church as a whole has rightly tried to raise the barriers to any kind of war as high as possible. Modern weapons are so destructive and the potential for civilian casualties so great that the decision to use force is surrounded with responsibilities more grave than ever. Some distinctions, however, have developed, even since the U.S. Bishops' Pastoral Letter on War and Peace in 1983, when, in the context of the Cold War, mutual deterrence was judged morally necessary because of the threat of nuclear obliteration. Now, we've been told, even nuclear weapons can be discriminate; they don't have to be total. Perhaps the possibility of waging a just war, a war using weaponry in a very discriminate way, is more at hand than ever. The progression in weapon technologies makes it both harder to justify going to war, because the potential destruction is so much greater, and also easier to justify pursuing war because *we can discriminate,* we can often target combatants alone.

The Church, in her social teaching, continues to uphold the possibility of just war. The proper reluctance to use force should not make us any less certain that, in a fallen world, there are times when only a just use of force will fulfill our responsibilities for protecting others. There are, however, two important positions opposed to the Church's just war tradition. One is a pacifist tradition, in which the use of force is never permitted. This position holds that a disciple of Jesus Christ may not go to war in any circumstance. The other is a militarist position that would say, once the decision is made to go to war, get it done on war's own terms. War is not a moral act anyway, so it's ridiculous to talk about the moral conditions for waging a war justly. In this view, called "realism," war is at best a necessary evil for a justifiable end. Contrary to both pacifism and "moral realism," the basic assumption underlying just war theory is that war is undesirable and should never be undertaken unless absolutely necessary, but war remains a human activity that can be judged by the same moral principles that govern all human acts. The theory is in fact an effort to prevent or to diminish warfare, for people are going to be killed in any war. But if war cannot or should not be avoided, then the theory seeks to restrict its horrors by establishing rigorous conditions that help determine what means of warfare are permissible and what are not.

Many wars are recognizably immoral: wars of pure aggression, wars of revenge or retribution, wars of unjust land annexation. None of these can fulfill the conditions for just warfare. To go to war, there must first of all be just cause, that is, a real and certain danger to people who have a right to live their lives in peace. Innocent life has to be threatened; the conditions necessary for decent human existence must be in imminent danger; fundamental human rights must be trampled upon. Second, competent authority has to make the decision to go to war. The right to use force is always joined to the common good; therefore, those who are primarily responsible for the common good, and they alone, may declare war. They have the basic obligation to evaluate the moral legitimacy of using force in given circumstances. Such judgments by the public authority are always subject to differences of opinion, but this fact does not of itself disqualify them or invalidate their binding force. A legitimate government has a right to determine that a country must go to war, and that decision is assumed to be morally binding. Public authority also includes now any legitimate and effective international authority, such as the United Nations has become over the last two generations.

That recognition brings into question national sovereignty in a global civilization. A nation or people is not fully sovereign if it has no right to declare war. Think of the states in our federal union. Think of colonies. If individual nations lose the right to declare war without reference to the United Nations, the fact and the understanding of national sovereignty shift. There's a great difference between our self-understanding of our sovereignty in this nation and the way the Holy See would approach the question of war and peace today. Along with many international jurists, the Vatican Secretariat of State assumes that the United Nations must now be involved in any morally legitimate decision to go to war. The common good of humanity as a whole is joined in a global society. Today, if any nation goes to war, it will affect all nations. Therefore, some kind of global institution, imperfect though it might be, as is the United Nations, is necessary as a point of reference for deciding when the conditions for a just war are satisfied. Even the UN Charter, however, recognizes the right of member states to defend themselves.

A just cause, a declaration by competent authority, and, third, consideration of the costs and risks involved are necessary in judging the morality of a war. Do all the rights and values involved justify the maiming, the violence, and the killing if force is used, even in a conflict that in itself might be justified? Would the end result be the same or worse whether or not a nation went to war? In short, is a war worth it? There's also the fact that no state is likely to have absolute justice on its side. All thinking people will hesitate to claim that a given conflict is absolutely justified. No nation at war can be absolutely sure, even as its armed forces are engaged in warfare, that God is with them in all they do.

Fourth, as in every moral action, there has to be right intention if a nation is conducting a just war. Does a government intend the good or is something more base driving it to war? The legitimate reasons for the use of violence are self-defense and the pursuit of lasting peace and reconciliation. Revenge or the attempt to expand one's own country's sphere of influence are not legitimate reasons for the use of force. The fifth condition for going to war justly is that military force remains the last resort, after all peaceful alternatives have been explored and found wanting. Both Pope John Paul II and Pope Benedict XVI have appealed to international organizations to reform themselves so that their structures and their activities give them the ability to uphold world order. In the economic order, international organizations seem incapable of controlling the dynamics of a seemingly anonymous market, with the result that all people do not presently benefit from economic development. In the political order, there is no global government, and, in fact, few think one desirable. The Pope isn't saying that full-scale global government is desirable as such, but he is saying that global international political institutions should develop so that international law can qualify or control the declaration and conditions of warfare between nation-states.

To have a just war, therefore, there must be a just cause; competent authority must decide to wage war for the common good; risks must have been evaluated and the end result be deemed worse if a nation doesn't go to war; the government must have a right intention; war must be the last resort; and, finally, the use of force must have a reasonable probability of success and the costs incurred be proportionate to the good achieved. If there's no possibility of bringing to a peaceful conclusion this exercise in force, then a nation has no right to use it. Statecraft must seek to defend and advance the prospects for peace. The purpose of going to war is to achieve a lasting peace, a just peace; if that's not possible, if violence will continue without any kind of resolution that will permit a hope of peace, then there is no right to go to war. If all these criteria are met (and they're not easily met, as one can see by rehearsing them in one's own mind), a nation may employ force in the face of an aggressor nation. At times, it may have a moral obligation to do so to protect its people.

Once a war is considered morally legitimate, another set of criteria comes into play. How is war to be conducted so that it continues to be morally justified? Going to war involves making decisions that presuppose some knowledge of strategy and tactics, weaponry and military planning. It takes expertise to follow the conflict. At a certain point, a concern for morality in pursuing warfare might cause the nation at war to limit, suspend, or conclude hostilities. This seems to be effectively what happened during the Vietnam War when the U.S. Catholic bishops recognized at first that South Vietnam had a right to exist as an independent nation and a right to call upon us to help them to exist; but when the conflict reached such levels of devastation not only in Vietnam but also in the damage inflicted on the common good in our own society, torn apart as it was by the conduct of this war, the bishops judged that the moral justification for the continuance of the war had ceased. They asked our government to negotiate peace without abandoning those who had trusted that we would keep our promises to them. The two sides of the request could not, in fact, be realized.

The first criterion, therefore, in talking about the *jus in bello,* the right way of conducting a war justly or morally, is proportionality. This means that the response to an initial aggression must not be greater than the aggression itself. If the conflict should escalate, the parties may find themselves in total warfare. No use, therefore, of chemical, bacteriological, or nuclear weapons can be justified. In 1983, the U.S. bishops said the possession of nuclear weapons as a deterrent is morally justified, but their use is always immoral. In a sense, the bishops justified playing a game of bluff, because atomic weapons cannot function as a deterrent if a potential enemy does not believe they will be used. Even though newer nuclear weapons can discriminate in their destructive power more carefully than in the past, using them now would be crossing a threshold that would open the world to such enormous danger that their use would be morally wrong.

The second criterion for conducting a war justly is discrimination in the use of force. Noncombatants cannot be the intended targets of harm. A just response to aggression must be directed against aggressors, not against innocent people caught up in a war not of their own making. It is likely that, in any conflict, civilians will fall in harm's way, but it is morally forbidden to knowingly and maliciously target them. That being said, it is hard to scrutinize a conflict in progress because any government will try to influence public opinion to support the war effort.

I was a very young child in Chicago during the Second World War. I remember that we had to buy black window shades so enemy planes could not see our house in case of an air attack. Chicago, at that time, given the limitations of fighter planes, was not in danger of an attack from the German or Japanese air force. But we still went through these civil defense exercises. We were instructed to turn off all house lights, except in the room with the blackout shade. My father, too old to be drafted, was an air raid warden. He had a metal helmet and a gas mask that I used to look at occasionally in the closet, and he would have to go out on nights when there was a civil defense blackout. They would drop crepe paper streamers; and the next morning, we children would go out and pick them up. The streamers represented bombs. If you discovered a streamer next to your house, you knew your house had been bombed. All of this had less to do with protecting Chicago than with bringing the conflict and its danger home to people thousands of miles away from the theater of war. These exercises made the danger of war very real. They fortified support for the war effort, and they combated American, especially midwestern, isolationism. They were propaganda exercises, for a just cause, but they were manipulations designed to make us in Chicago, in the middle of the continent, recognize that we were involved in the struggle, as well. And they worked.

In the nature of things, a government will do everything it can to unite its people around the war effort. Therefore, it's very difficult for a private citizen to judge that proportionality is violated, and the weapons being used are indiscriminate in their targets. Moral arguments about the right to go to war can be made before a war begins, but, once a nation is engaged in conflict, as one knows even from interpersonal conflict, it's much harder to step back and make moral judgments.

Because of the intricacies of just war theory and because war of any kind is such a dangerous and terrible thing, devastating the life and the well-being of individuals and societies, brutalizing those who fight in it, and often destructive of civilized values, pacifism seems to have clear superiority as a moral choice. Morally serious people can get impatient and say, "You bishops have your just war theory, but it's a speculative game. In fact, the only real moral response is pacifism. That's the only way to avoid implication in sin and to be sure you are acting with God." To this reaction, just war theory holds that a war can be moral, and it can be fought morally as well.

The Church recognizes pacifism as a legitimate and even heroic position for individuals. It does not, however, recognize pacifism as a legitimate position for governments, because governments have the obligation to protect their own innocent citizens and to safeguard the common good even by force, if force becomes necessary. Pacifism is something like celibacy: it's a radical call from Christ to individuals, but if everybody heard such a call, normal society would disappear! The realm of the properly secular world would be inappropriately sacralized. Nonetheless, we need celibates and we need pacifists. Just as people are called to celibacy by Christ for the sake of the Kingdom, where everyone will, in fact, be celibate, where there will be no marriage or giving in marriage, so also there are people called by Christ to give witness to the peace of God's Kingdom, to be pacifist in the strict sense, and to live with all the consequences of that vocation. Pacifism is a way of witnessing to the power of God, the Kingdom of God inchoatively present here and now. We should be grateful to people who are willing to undertake that kind of witness, even though we recognize it is not a position that can govern the conduct of nations. Those who are pacifists and are Christians usually argue that the teaching of Christ rules out recourse to any kind of violence. It is true that the teaching of Christ excludes the seeking of revenge and calls for rebuilding damaged relationships through forgiveness. This is how God deals with us, and it is how those who have become God's children ought to act. It entails peacemaking, reconciliation, overcoming of opposition by love on the part of individuals and societies. But neither individuals nor societies are enjoined against ever taking up arms against an enemy of the common good; such a prohibition would abandon the world to the forces of evil. God can and does save his people, but a God who respects our freedom acts through human beings to achieve his will on earth.

Pacifism arises from a particular religious and moral vision that has an honored place in Christian life. For some, Christian life is a *fuga mundi,* a flight from the world. That's the vision that guided the desert fathers after the Roman persecutions ended. That is the vision that inspires, to some extent, those in consecrated life. There is always in consecrated life a distancing of oneself from the world for the sake of giving witness, in this world, to a world yet to come. But that is not the calling of everyone who follows Jesus Christ. Lay faithful participate in the mission of Christ to save both persons and societies by recognizing that, at times, the tranquillity of order needs to be defended, for enemies are very real. We wouldn't be called upon to forgive if we didn't have real enemies. At times, in order to meet the enemy, one must resort to force.

We have had particularly impressive witnesses in our day to various sorts of pacifism. These witnesses became the prophets who call us constantly, even as we struggle with just war theory, to be witnesses to the peace that is the gift of Christ. Pope John Paul II stressed the effectiveness of nonviolence in confronting injustice in the world without ruling out the possible need to use force as a last resort. The most spectacular nonviolent witnesses of recent generations have been Mahatma Gandhi against the British in India and Martin Luther King, Jr., in the civil rights struggles in the United States. But these nonviolent struggles were in contexts where one could expect a moral response from the individual or the state or institution to which one was giving nonviolent witness. In the context of the English imperium in India, in the context of our own constitutional order, nonviolence is an effective means to work toward justice; and it succeeded in those two cases. It never worked in the Soviet Union, because the government response to nonviolence there was not a measured response respectful of human rights. It was simply to destroy those who were trying to be nonviolent in their protest against the injustice that lay at the heart of the Soviet project.

We respect and honor those who take the pacifist option. For some individuals, it's a heroic thing to do, and we all benefit from their witness. But Christians in some carefully defined, limited, and self-critical circumstances may make use of the just war option as formulated by St. Augustine and developed in Catholic social teaching in loving obedience to God. It takes great courage and firmness in sacrifice to engage in a limited and controlled use of force, saying no to some kinds of war and to some actions within a just war, refusing to obliterate the enemy, working with the will to accept defeat rather than to allow the war to become total. This approach entails its own kind of heroism and its own type of courage and bravery. The 1983 U.S. bishops' pastoral letter made the point that analysis from the perspective of total nonviolence and analysis from the perspective of just war teaching sometimes converge in their opposition to methods of warfare. I think the writing of that letter was the first occasion for our episcopal conference to discuss Christian pacifism, even as the bishops supported just war theory.

Having accepted the principles of just war theory, can we

recognize particular contemporary challenges to it? There are at least four major obstacles to the use of just war theory today in governing the use of force by nation-states.

First of all, terrorism as we experience it now is a challenge to just war theory, because the enemy is not a sovereign state. The enemy is a movement. It is a well-organized group, as Pope John Paul II pointed out in his message for the 2002 World Day of Peace. There is an international terrorist network, and it is very effective. It isn't sovereign, and it doesn't make any claim to sovereignty. It claims, at times, a religious justification. What was most chilling about the attacks of September 11, 2001, was their being done in the name of the God of Abraham. To attack innocent people without provocation in the name of God is not just an act of terrorism; it's an act of blasphemy. As religious believers we have to ask how it is possible that "religion" would be used to justify such violence. Pope John Paul II kept repeating that religions are to be part of the solution to violence, not its cause. In 2002, he outlined something of the philosophy and the spirit that motivates terrorism. He said, "Those who kill by acts of terrorism actually despair of humanity, of life, of the future. Such action springs from the conviction that everything is to be hated and destroyed."[5] The Holy Father points out that terrorism founds itself on contempt for human life and is a horrible parody of religion, which, at its heart, is to glorify God and his creation. In resorting to terror, one commits a crime against humanity and against God.

No matter the motivation for terrorism, it presents no sovereign nation as opponent, and one of the criteria for a just war therefore seems inapplicable. How can one conduct a just war when there is no visible opponent who is engaged according to the rules of warfare? Terrorism doesn't give itself to dialogue, which would permit one to determine whether war is really justified. To whom does one send the declaration of war? To whom or with whom does one negotiate? How can one work through the set of moral criteria for going to war when the invader, the aggressor, is anonymous or hidden, when there are no means of contact? In fact, it's impossible to enter into negotiations with terrorists; one can only say that, when it is clear that an attack has been made, one has a right to self-defense.

Gauging the morality of a response to given acts of terrorism is complicated because of the transnational character of contemporary terrorism. The existence of organized international terrorism expresses the weakness or even the failure of modern states. There are failed nation-states in some parts of the world and ineffective nation-states elsewhere. Inability to identify the terrorist movement with particular states doesn't mean one can't defend oneself against it. It does, however, pose the difficulty of determining how to identify the guilty parties with reasonable certitude. Criminal culpability is personal. It cannot be extended to a whole nation, ethnic group, or religion, even if terrorists belong to a particular nation, ethnic group, or religion. How does one pinpoint the enemy one wants to forgive as well as to fight? The only solution, according to the Holy Father, is some kind of international cooperation in the fight against terrorist activities. This cooperation in discovering terrorists must include a courageous and resolute political and economic commitment to relieving situations of oppression that are used to justify the designs of terrorists. The difficulty in determining exactly who is responsible for a terrorist threat is a contemporary challenge to using just war theory to coordinate a war on terrorism.

The second challenge to just war theory comes from the notion of humanitarian intervention, as was experienced in recent years in Bosnia, Somalia, Rwanda, East Timor, Kosovo, and Sudan. Humanitarian military intervention brings the international community into a nation in order to save people from their own government or from a civil war or genocide. If there is genocide, the international community has the obligation to intervene, even against a sovereign state. But the decision making can be complicated by lack of adequate information and by the sometimes inadequate presupposition of just war theory itself: violence against a sovereign state is unjust unless that sovereign state has invaded another country, not because it is killing its own people.

An argument for humanitarian intervention presupposes that the United Nations and its agencies are effective means of international mediation and intervention. As a matter of fact, the effectiveness of the UN has been and is still severely limited. The ideal would be that, either through the United Nations or through other organizations, nation-states could cooperate in the punishment of rogue states that are destroying their own people. The United States has a particular moral obligation to raise the question of rules to govern humanitarian intervention because we claim moral justification for our international military actions, and we are able to act when some of the international institutions that should be in place default.

The third area that challenges classical just war theory is nuclear policy. That topic was officially addressed by the American bishops in 1983 in the context of the Cold War. But the world is now beyond the Cold War, and therefore the question of the use of nuclear weaponry as a deterrent must again be raised. One has to ask, What kind of defense could morally permit the crossing of the nuclear threshold and the risk of total war? It would seem that, in terms of classical just war theory, even the most discriminate use of nuclear weapons would create such risks that their possession should now be judged immoral.

Fourth and last, the Iraq War raised the challenge of a preemptive strike. In just war theory, one may strike a country that is poised to invade, but the threat of Iraqi invasion of the United States was not imminent. Nonetheless, in the aftermath of September 11, 2001, the danger of turning a blind eye to the probability of savage and indiscriminate violence by terrorists anywhere was undeniable. Could just war theory therefore allow a preemptive strike on Iraq? Saddam Hussein had not openly threatened to use force against our country. Of course, Iraq's practical refusal to allow thorough inspection of its weapons sites and the apparent discovery of new sites for building and launching nuclear weapons seemed to indicate a threat. But Saddam kept playing the card of being open to further inspections. The judgment was that he was using cooperation as a ploy, and perhaps he was. But just war theory says that one must take all steps possible to avoid war, even if they don't promise much success.

What then was the moral status of the preemptive strike made by President George W. Bush with the majority backing of Congress? Protection of our citizens was the reason the government had to say that we were going to fight terrorists after September 11, but certain conditions must be in place before launching a preemptive strike. These were brought out by Bishop Wilton Gregory, president of the U.S. Conference of Catholic Bishops at the time, in his letter to President Bush. Intelligence agencies of our government and other nations needed proof that Saddam had in some way contributed to worldwide terrorism and that he had every intent of wreaking havoc on our citizens or on other nations once he acquired the necessary weapons, especially nuclear and biological weapons, to conduct total war. The case had also to be made that he was directly connected to the attacks on our country of September 11, or that he would, if he had the necessary weapons, be involved in attacks in the future. If such evidence had been forthcoming, then, knowing that all avenues to dissuade him from terrorism and from implementing any kind of evil action against our citizens had been exhausted, military force would have been the only remaining option to protect the world.

To be morally justified, however, a plan of attack against the Iraqi regime would have had to be so carefully thought out that it would use only as much military force as necessary to achieve its purpose: the defeat of terrorism. All our military efforts would have been directed at toppling Saddam's regime with the minimal amount of damage and loss of life on both sides. Every effort would have been made to protect innocent Iraqis from harm. These concerns certainly influenced the initial planning of the war. Once Saddam's regime was eliminated, plans would have had to be implemented to support the Iraqi people themselves in forming a government of their choice and in helping that government provide for the needs of its citizens. Congress and the American people would have had to give their support to such an undertaking. Here, obviously, things have gone awry. The judgment of the U.S. bishops at the time of the Iraq invasion was that the evidence to justify a preemptive strike against Iraq was not available and the conditions for just war were not met.

Further, the obligations we incurred to the Iraqi people because we invaded their nation have not been met. Iraqi citizens' right to live in peace in their own country was not adequately secured during the years of occupation, and they are still not secured even as the U.S. military leaves Iraq. The last state is as bad as, if not worse than, the first, at least for Iraqi religious minorities, especially Christians.

Pope John Paul II was a persistent voice on behalf of non-violent solutions, but he also called for humanitarian intervention and for peacekeeping operations in various other trouble spots in the world, as has Pope Benedict XVI. Their advocacy of humanitarian intervention to disarm an aggressor, as much as their praise for nonviolence, is contributing to a rethinking of the Catholic position on the use of force in world affairs. Because a nation has a right to defend itself against global terrorism, just war theory has had to broaden its concerns beyond warfare between sovereign states. But the right to self-defense and the defense of others is not the heart of the Gospel message. The right to defense, for those interested in bringing good out of evil, has to be read in the context of forgiveness. Forgiving our enemies brings us to the heart of God's action in the world.

The pillars of peace are justice and forgiveness. The last defenses against terrorism are the justice that seeks to ensure full respect for rights and responsibilities, assuring the equitable distribution of benefits and burdens; and the forgiveness that heals and rebuilds troubled human relations from their foundations. The goal is not an imposed peace that is only the absence of war but a healing of relationships so that we can live together in mutual respect and even in friendship across national and cultural boundaries.

To make friends of enemies demands mutual forgiveness. With forgiveness, another coefficient has been brought into the moral equation that is just war doctrine. Forgiveness doesn't figure directly in traditional just war thinking, but John Paul II, speaking to world religious leaders in 2002, said that we commit ourselves to forgiving one another for past and present errors and prejudices, and to supporting one another in a common effort to overcome selfishness and arrogance, hatred and violence, vindictiveness and revenge. We have learned from the past that peace without justice is no true peace, but just relations cannot be solidly restored without mutual forgiveness. Forgiveness begins as a personal choice, a decision of the heart to go against the natural instinct to pay back evil with evil; forgiveness then becomes a social reality that goes well beyond its beginnings in the human heart. The Holy Father's hope was that an ethics and culture of forgiveness could prevail, bringing into being a politics of forgiveness that will be expressed in society's attitudes and laws.

Pope Benedict returned to the theme of reconciliation after the 2009 Synod for Africa, in an address to the Roman Curia:

> One might say that reconciliation and justice are the two essential premises of peace and that, therefore, to a certain extent, they also define its nature. Let us limit ourselves to the word "reconciliation." A mere glance at the sufferings and sorrows of recent history in Africa, but also in many other parts of the world, shows that unresolved and deeply rooted disputes can in some situations cause outbreaks of violence in which every trace of humanity seems to disappear. Peace can only be achieved as the result of inner

reconciliation. We may consider the history of Europe following the Second World War as a positive example of a process of reconciliation that is succeeding. The fact that since 1945 there have been no more wars in Western and Central Europe has without a doubt been due primarily to wise and ethically oriented political and economic structures, but these were only able to develop because of the prior existence of inner processes of reconciliation which made possible a new coexistence. Every society needs acts of reconciliation in order to enjoy peace. These acts are a prerequisite of a good political order, but they cannot be achieved by politics alone. They are pre-political processes and they must spring from other sources.[6]

This perspective is challenging for Americans, because culturally we are often determinists in our understanding of human behavior. We seem to find it difficult to believe that people can change, can convert. The Church, however, acts with the help of God's grace, which makes radical conversion, complete change, possible because Jesus has risen from the dead and makes everything new.

In conversations about the sacrament of reconciliation with priests of the Archdiocese of Chicago, some observed, "Our people have lost a sense of sin." But others replied, "No, not at all. We have a very highly developed sense of sin and even a highly developed sense of confession." We have in U.S. religious history tent meetings, where people publicly confessed their sins. We have the equivalent of that confession now on television talk shows, where people boast of the most horrendous actions. They and we know intuitively what's wrong and what's right. We have a sense of sin. We even have a sense of confession of sin. One younger priest then said, "What we've forgotten is forgiveness. We really don't know how to forgive."

He couldn't have been more correct. We acknowledge guilt, but many of us can't forgive or believe that forgiveness is possible. Forgiveness is an activity proper to God, and it is forgiveness that displays the power of God, the presence of God.

Experiencing the forgiveness that comes from Christ's redeeming sacrifice for our salvation leads one to qualify just war theory as it has come to us in its classical form. The Church is saying that families, groups, societies, states, and the international community itself need to forgive their enemies in order to move beyond the sterility of mutual condemnation and political stalemate. The ability to forgive lies at the basis of hope for a society marked by justice and solidarity. Because we believe it can be morally permissible to defend oneself with force, we also have to point out that, as Christians, we can do so only if we forgive our enemies. Only then are we at work with God, whose nature is to love with an eagerness to forgive.

7

COMMERCE AS A SUBSTITUTE FOR WAR: BUSINESS AS A VOCATION FROM GOD

Over three centuries ago, as the modern nation-state and the capitalist economic order developed, it was hoped that "sweet commerce" would replace warfare as the moral way to contain human competition. States with developed economies would not go to war because war would interfere with business. In fact, trade wars show that commercial activity can cause conflicts as often as it might prevent them. For those engaged commercially, however, seeing business as a vocation, a personal calling and not just a livelihood, keeps economic activity centered on virtues that unite businesspeople to God and to his designs for the world.

In 2004, *The New York Times Magazine* featured a cover story titled "With God at Our Desks: The Rise of Religion and Evangelism in the American Workplace." Russell Shorto, who wrote it, described this faith-at-work movement as a reaction to the separation of God from everyday life: "The idea is that Christians have for too long practiced their faith on Sundays and left it behind during the workweek, that there is a moral vacuum in the modern workplace, which leads to backstabbing careerism, empty routines for employees and CEOs who push for profits at the expense of society, the environment and their fellow human beings."[1]

The separation of faith from the ordinary affairs of life is not a new problem for believers. St. Paul talks about bringing all things together into one, through Christ. Life itself, in Christianity and in any revealed religion, is a call from God to live with him forever. But in living our life, in doing diverse things, in pursuing one activity and one goal after another, life ends up more compartmentalized than unified. Does it have to be so?

There is marriage and family, and its obligations and joys; there is work and business; the obligations of citizenship; social clubs; sports life, leisure activities. Each of these can be considered a compartment. When one divides one's life up among them, there are requirements for this and standards for that, and there are ways to check whether one is coming up to the standards. A person can go through life filling in the blanks correctly, living up to all the requirements as well as possible, but in the end still not understand who he or she truly is. Life doesn't come together adequately, and, after a while, ennui develops. A certain "quiet desperation" may set in because people can't fit their lives together. They can't see life as a calling that points to the hope, behind every particular action, for a good life here with the promise of an eternal destiny. Can business be seen as part of that larger calling, as something worthy of that calling, something that contributes to it, something that in itself is noble, something that contributes to holiness, to sanctification, to cooperation with God?

A famous epistle to Diognetus addresses the problems of separating faith from life; it was perhaps written by St. Justin,

who was martyred in Rome around A.D. 150. He was a teacher
of philosophy before he converted to Christianity; and, when he
converted, he looked upon Christianity as a philosophy, indeed
as *the* philosophy, that is, as an integrated way of living. St. Paul,
of course, talked about discipleship as an integrated way of living. In Judaism, Moses gave a way of life from God himself that
mediated every dimension of human experience through God's
law for his people. Religion is something that's total in itself and
can therefore permeate business and every dimension of human
activity. The *Letter to Diognetus* put it this way:

> For Christians are not distinguished from the rest of
> mankind either in locality or in speech or in customs.
> They dwell not somewhere in cities of their own, neither
> do they use some different language, nor practice an ex-
> traordinary kind of life. They dwell in their own coun-
> tries, but always as sojourners; they bear their share in all
> things as citizens, and they endure all hardships as strang-
> ers. Every foreign country is a fatherland to them, and
> every fatherland is foreign. They marry like all other men
> and they beget children; but they do not cast away their
> offspring. They have their meals in common, but not their
> wives. They find themselves in the flesh, and yet they live
> not after the flesh. Their existence is on earth, but their
> citizenship is in heaven. They obey the established laws,
> and they surpass the laws in their own lives.
>
> In a word, what the soul is in a body, disciples of Christ
> are to be in the world. The soul is spread through all the
> members of the body, and Christians through the diverse
> cities of the world. The soul has its abode in the body, and

yet it is not of the body. So Christians have their abode in the world, and yet they are not of the world.[2]

Revealed religion is a gift that calls us to something beyond what and who we presently are. In fact, religion turns us inside out. It converts us. Hearing a call is always difficult because it means change, and most of us think everybody else ought to change, but not us. The Pope should change, the Church should change, my mother-in-law should change, but I don't need to change at all. Resistance to change instantly arises when one tries to convince people they should do something they didn't think of themselves. In daily life, clashes arise when faith says one thing and the country's way of life or culture says something different. If the clash is great enough, believers end up a persecuted minority. Most of us would like to be able to live our lives in peace. Nonetheless, the distinction between the demands of faith and cultural mores is there, and necessarily so. Our culture is our own creation and our call is from God, who isn't our creature. There's bound to be tension built into a life that is supposed to be integrated by faith but has to be lived out in many circles that aren't much influenced by that faith. Yet it is in the midst of that tension that we are to find God at work. God is light, which is why he wants to enter into the shadows of strife. He acts to illuminate the boxes of our busyness.

At present, our way of handling the problem of compartmentalization in a secularized society is to divide public from private. The public realm is secular, and the private realm gives space for religious sentiments, whatever they might be; but one is not to cross the line between the public and the private or confuse public issues by introducing religious considerations in judging them. That isn't, however, the way our country started, nor is it a way to pursue freedom in action. There's a distinction and a separation in law between religious institutions and political institutions, but not between faith and society; the first 150 years of this country's history bear witness to healthy interaction between the concerns of society and the influence of faith. What has developed now, however, is the gradual establishment of profane secularism as the public "religion." What is public is secular, and religious sentiments can be entertained only privately. This solution is temporary and unsatisfactory; people cannot indefinitely live parallel lives. Dissipated by contrary claims, at the end of the day and perhaps at the end of our lives, we're not quite sure who we are. Worse, one way of life will work to rid the world of the other. A house divided cannot stand, as both Abraham Lincoln and Sacred Scripture tell us.

Different theories explain why integrating our lives seems especially challenging now. The Trappist monk Thomas Merton talked about false selves. He said these selves are like the masks worn by actors in Greek tragedies, masks we don when interacting with others. We adopt a persona, a role that we feel others want us to play. There is the "family mask," the "friend mask," the "business mask," the "boss mask," the "pious mask," and so forth. We even speak of a mask for our recreation in the form of a "game face." We are so busy trying to discover and generate the kind of self we think others want us to be that our real selves— made in the image and likeness of God—may become lost or obscured. The psychic energy expended in donning these different masks is quite demanding.

Merton says we do this as a form of protection, because we believe that if people *really* knew who we are, if they really knew our authentic selves, we would not "measure up." We wouldn't be found "lovable." So we try to create the person we think others want us to be. This endeavor of course means not only that our faith fails to integrate our personal life but also that our faith can't affect the larger life, the culture itself, the society. Merton asserts that the way to begin to integrate, to bring things back together, is to spend enough time with the Lord. In his presence, we put aside the lie that we don't measure up, that we're not lovable. The One who knows us best is also the One who loves us most, and we discover what he thinks of us and how he loves us by spending some time daily in prayer. Without time spent with God, we'll not know who we are in his sight. Then the possibility of our faith integrating everything else is lost, and we'll go through life believing that, no matter how successful we've been in various spheres, we don't in the end prove adequate to life itself.

God's unending and merciful love, discovered and lived as that factor in life that unifies everything else, including our work, will make us integrated persons, people free to act authentically. Once one makes the shift to accept the love of God in its infinite mercy and to reject the process of creating and projecting false selves, then gradually, day after day, one's life becomes more unified.

There are specific challenges proper to the vocation of businesspeople as they work toward integrating their lives around a sense of calling. What is proper to business leaders, as opposed to actors or firefighters or teachers or priests? Those who see business as a vocation understand that, through their work, they sanctify themselves and help make the world a place where others can find their sanctification, can live with the Lord. They take to heart what Christ said about his disciples: You are to be salt of the earth and light of the world. We are to be disciples of the Lord in good times and in bad. Jesus also talks about the leaven in the dough that raises everything up. Businesspeople with a sense of vocation want to achieve more than just getting the work done according to the standards and the protocols of a company and the requirements of professional associations. Their work brings them into partnership with the Lord, but how?

Work creates community and it serves community. No one works completely alone. People are brought together, forming a type of community that creates something for the service of society through efficiently using capital and labor and by enabling all to be better stewards of God's creation, which has been given to our care. Business provides numerous ways for men and women to exercise their duty to others and their desire to be creative and productive. The marketplace, in a sound business climate, stimulates people to exercise the virtue of industriousness. In the challenges of economic initiative, entrepreneurial abilities are developed. Business provides necessary goods and services, and companies usually give contributions from their profits to other organizations, for the good of civil society. Through business activities, the wealth of investors and of society as a whole is increased, and possibilities for greater sharing are therefore multiplied.

All of this is good. But is there an order of importance? Yes, and it starts with the community created. Modern business manuals abound with the advice that the best companies in the long run are the ones that respect and care for their employees. But that's just a reflection of the deeper truth that we were created by God as social beings. God created a couple in the very beginning, and Christians believe that God himself is a Trinity, a community of three divine persons in one God. We come from community and we are created for community. The interpersonal communion established and enhanced in the activity of work is therefore more important than the product that is produced. It doesn't look that way in the financial reports, but experience teaches that creating and nurturing interpersonal relationships is crucial to business success. A CEO can't be friends, can't have an I-thou relationship, with eighteen thousand employees. None-theless, there is a company atmosphere or family culture; the best companies, those that have a common sense of purpose, are places where the spirit of the company is more than the sum total of the individuals who work there. The workers feel they're contributing to a common enterprise, which serves the common good of society itself. In the whole experience, prioritizing has to start with this concern for community.

Work is also a basic form of self-expression; even though it's not art as such, it is a form of artistic creation, because work is creative. Without it, we wouldn't discover who we are by producing something that reflects ourselves back to us. It's a misinterpretation of the book of Genesis to regard work as a curse, as consequent upon mankind's falling into sin. Work predates the fall in Scripture. Adam and Eve were to till and care for the garden. They were called by God to name the animals, to take custody of the earth, and that meant work. The difference is that, after sin entered human history, nature shared in man's fall, and now our work is hindered by our own selfishness and nature's cross-purposes. Now we have to struggle against the tendency toward concupiscence, which leads to vices such as sloth and greed. But work itself is not a curse; it's a God-like service, even when toilsome. We work in imitation of God's creative activity, and we rest when that activity is over. The activity is good not just because of what it produces but because it's simply good to work. If this were not true, business could not be seen as a vocation. It would be no more than a way to make money, so that people can then do what they really want to do, expressing who they really are in the time off from work. That is, again, to compartmentalize our lives between who we really are in private, on our own time, and the public demands of work.

Work as a form of self-expression is different from the self-expression one finds in family or faith, but, nonetheless, our faith itself tells us that, in working, we cooperate with God in constantly re-creating the world. For a believer, work is seen as a participation in God's plan for the development of the world, cooperating with the establishment of God's Kingdom, which is, finally, eternal, but which has seeds here in our experience. Pope John Paul II talks in his *Letter on Human Work* (*Laborem exercens,* 1981) about work being part of the Creator's original ordering. Faith gives a motive to work; it also enables us to see the working itself as imitating the purpose and activity of God. Work is part of establishing ourselves as God's creatures, laboring in line with his purpose and establishing goals to achieve what is good for ourselves and others.

Not only does work create a community, not only does work help us to express ourselves, but work also contributes to human history. The modern economy is the cause of the wealth of nations. Human ingenuity, creativity, and organizational genius have enabled mankind to create developed societies that now, in a global economy, are beginning to transform the entire world in unforeseen ways. Human beings keep discovering better ways of using the resources of the earth to meet human needs. It isn't only war and politics that create the history of the human race; it is work itself and particularly the modern business economy that has been a major actor in transforming human history. It's more dramatic in the history books to talk about kings and generals than it is to talk about CEOs and union leaders. But as we reread human history, not just in the last century or two but even back much further, we see how it is work and work as structured into corporations or other forms of organizing labor and capital in society that is one of the primary ways to comprehend the dynamics of human history. Businesses contribute to the building up of the history of the human race, within particular political, ethical, and legal frameworks. Business is a vocation, a calling to goods higher than the financial.

There are, of course, important criticisms of the modern business economy, especially in the wake of the collapse in recent years of many financial institutions. Religious people sometimes talk as if there were something wrong in making a profit, but the alternative to making a profit is going bankrupt. There are exorbitant profits and there are exorbitant salaries, but the legitimate role of profit, according to Pope John Paul II in his *Letter on Human Work,* is as an indication that a business is functioning well. When a firm makes a profit, productive factors have been properly used and corresponding human needs have been duly satisfied.

John Paul II goes on to say that profitability is not the only indicator of a firm's condition. It is possible for the financial accounts to be in order, and yet the people who make up the firm's most valuable asset, the community of workers mentioned earlier, are regularly humiliated and their dignity offended. Besides being morally inadmissible, this situation will eventually have negative repercussions on the firm's economic efficiency. In fact, the purpose of a business firm is not simply to make a profit, legitimate and necessary though that is. The purpose is to exist as a community of persons who, in various ways, are endeavoring to satisfy their basic needs and who form a particular group at the service of the whole of society and of the common good. Human and moral factors that, in the long run, are at least as important as making a profit for the life of a business must always be considered. Benedict XVI wrote in his 2009 encyclical *Caritas in veritate* that true love for others "requires that shape and structure be given to those types of economic initiatives which, without rejecting profit, aim at a higher goal than the mere logic of the exchange of equivalents, of profit as an end in itself" (38). People demand respect more than they demand wages.

Other moral perils in pursuing business as a vocation come to mind. There are moral and social dangers associated with modern approaches to advertising when it makes false claims and instills sinful desires. There is the great problem of the distribution of wealth once it is generated. The continued gap between rich nations and poor nations, sixty-five years after the international financial protocols for development were worked out at the end of the Second World War, brings into question our present global economic order. There's also the problem of equity in corporate pay. The list goes on and on. Each of these issues has very technical dimensions, but they collectively demonstrate the human and moral context of economic production and exchange.

In our society, it seems that too many people have to work too many hours, and many families feel the need to have both parents work full-time, no matter how young their children.

United Nations studies in 2000 showed that the average American employee worked 137 hours (that's three and a half weeks) more per year than the average Japanese worker and 499 hours (an amazing twelve and a half added weeks per year) more than the average German worker. Neither the Japanese nor the Germans have the reputation of being lazy. These long hours did make us the most productive workers on earth per individual worker. We should note, however, that we are not the most productive workers per hour worked. In this category, the French and the Belgians surpass us.[3] Our productivity is purchased at the cost of long and seemingly ever-increasing hours of work. There are many reasons for this trend, not the least of which is the high marginal cost of hiring new full-time employees and providing them with health and other benefits.

The spiritual and psychological results of such "workaholism" are becoming more evident. We are so busy making a living that we don't have time for a life with others or with God. Volunteer hours are down; time for those voluntary organizations that make our culture so much richer is less available. Families are spending less and less time with each other. For some, the family meal has become only something remembered from the past. Some studies show that school-age children are spending less than half an hour a day with their parents. This phenomenon led Pope John Paul II to speak in his 1994 *Letter to Families* (*Gratissimam sane*) of many children in First World nations who are growing up as "orphans of living parents."

If what I have said about the importance of the subjective dimension of work is true, that it creates a community, that it enables us to express ourselves, that it contributes to human history, then attention has to be paid to what work and long work hours do to the workers. The subjective dimension, the workers themselves, is as important as the objective product; its neglect costs us more than we can afford. Everyone wants work to be rewarding and fulfilling, and work, therefore, should not remove from human workers time needed for family, play, religion, culture, friendship.

In Chicago, the archdiocese did a survey to discover why Catholics don't go to Sunday Mass. I thought that perhaps the reason was the sex abuse scandal, or the fact that some Catholics no longer believe in the moral teachings of the Church, or because a bishop or a priest or a sister or a deacon hurt them in some way. As it turns out, the single most important reason for not worshiping God is that they're just too busy, that the way we've organized our social life, our collective life, is to have five days for work, work that is full-time and engages both parents. That leaves two days for family life. Those two days are private; they are one's own to structure as one pleases. Religion becomes a kind of hobby or a pastime; it's no longer the integrating principle in one's experience of life. There are many reasons for this secularization of personal life, but certainly contributing to it is the immense amount of time people now spend working. Even our recreation is often organized as a form of work. The Little Leagues and many other forms of organized sports and play, good though they are intended to be, are activities to which children are sent during these two days that are supposed to be free. If children don't eat with their parents as a family, the Eucharistic meal in their parish family will seem ever more strange to their experience of life.

Catholic social teaching asks that the primary wage earner in every family earn enough to support the family; in other words, one's pay is ordered to supporting family life. In the United States, however, one is paid only for work done, not to strengthen family relationships. Giving family benefits in health care and other services is one way in which the demands of Catholic social teaching about wages can be met. Time off for meeting maternity or paternity obligations, recognition of religious observances, and various special arrangements to meet family emergencies also help create a business and work climate that recognizes the worker as more important than the work. Loyalty to companies is now attenuated in proportion as companies' commitment to their workers diminishes, and it is harder for workers to see their companies as extensions of family. These are added challenges in considering business and work as a vocation from God, but they do not hide the truth that business can be about God's work and not just our own.

Looking at the financial order to see God's hand at work, Pope Benedict XVI suggests that "gift" be its organizing principle.[4] In our life with God, all is gift. In business, economic contracts are measured by equal values exchanged; gifts enter into corporate life after the bottom line is figured. But what if gifts were figured in before the bottom line appeared? Since a gift is a commodity with a person attached, the community I have described in this chapter would be intrinsic to the financial activity that shapes business itself if its culture were a culture of gift. God's action in and through business activity would also be more clearly evident.

MIGRANTS: WITH WHOM DOES GOD TRAVEL?

The Church holds that the migrant is first of all a gift and not a problem. The Church has voiced this conviction, which derives from God's activity as creator, in different ways and in various forums during the last decades, in which we have experienced the increasing pace of migration flows everywhere on the planet. Recent popes have repeatedly affirmed the cultural and religious dignity of migrants, especially in the annual messages on the World Day of Migrants and Refugees. The Post-Synodal Apostolic Exhortation *Ecclesia in America* (65), a document created after the bishops of the Western Hemisphere met in Rome at the 1997 Synod for America, underlines the Christian dimension of the rich cultural and religious heritage of most migrants in America. The U.S. Conference of Catholic Bishops, in one of its most important documents on immigration, *Welcoming the Stranger Among Us: Unity in Diversity* (2000), states: "Both on parish and diocesan levels, the presence of brothers and sisters from different cultures should be celebrated as a gift to the Church." In other words, there is no doubt about how the Church's faith shapes her stand on issues of immigration and the mobility of peoples in our day.

Yet these extremely positive evaluations of migration are quite controversial. Many people in our country and many faithful in our churches disagree with the affirmation of the cultural and religious value of migrants. How should we deal with the tension this disagreement has caused, and is still causing, within our communities and in society as a whole? How should we concretely affirm and promote the migrant as a cultural treasure and a privileged protagonist of the Gospel? What does it mean, in practice, to make this assertion about a "gift" that is grounded in faith? This chapter will deal with this subject in three steps: first, by briefly analyzing our contemporary context, characterized by the dynamic of globalization; second, by listing some of the main challenges that must be faced, especially in the United States, in the effort to affirm the cultural and religious dignity of the migrant; and third, by suggesting a Catholic vision and some pastoral strategies that could help to address the issue in the light of faith.

A GLOBAL SOCIETY

"Globalization" is the term commonly used to describe the huge economic, cultural, political, and religious processes that are transforming the planet. Although more precise definitions of this phenomenon abound, basically it has to do with the world becoming more and more unified through dramatic progress in information technology and transportation. The development of computers and the World Wide Web allows for virtually instant exchange of information across national borders. The development of air transportation and the consistent drop in travel costs have dramatically influenced the movement of peoples around the world. Connected with these factors is the expansion of the economic and financial markets into even the most remote corners of the earth. These phenomena have created a set of new relationships that affect local cultures and traditions, which are now in competition with global fashions and products.

Local cultures cannot be seen as static, unchanging systems of meaning and ways of life, because as living human creations they are continually evolving under the pressure of internal dynamics and external, global factors. Local traditions clash with global fashions especially among young people in their own world. In a different context, the children of immigrants are caught between the culture of their friends and that of their family in a new world. Moreover, contact with a country left behind is also easier for immigrants today, enabling them to live in two countries almost simultaneously. Finally, and unfortunately, one cannot ignore in analyzing today's context the influence of international terrorism and the various reactions to it. No comprehensive analysis of the global cultural and religious situation can fail to take into account terrorism's radical effects on the world. The "war on terror" has been justified or disputed for various reasons, but in every analysis the terrorist is the "other," both culturally and religiously. Consequently, the immigrant, who is also "other," can be tarred too easily with the brush of terrorism, made the object of suspicion, or even assumed to be a criminal.

Some global developments, like the advances in modes of transportation and the expansion of markets, are themselves among the main causes of the increase in migration around the world, particularly during the latter part of the twentieth century and the beginning of the twenty-first. Because of these massive movements of peoples, some social scientists have called this the "age of migration." It is the migrants themselves and their children (the second generation of each immigrant wave) who embody, more than anybody else, these global processes. They most tangibly represent the increasing cultural diversity in most societies today, the very diversity that causes the controversy and mixed feelings just noted. In the host societies, people wonder: Is this cultural diversity that we are experiencing a blessing or a curse? Is it an obstacle to the development of peoples or a treasure contributing to a richer future for humanity? Is it a threat to identity or a source of enrichment and renewal? The different answers given to these questions help clarify the challenges we face in affirming the cultural and religious worth of migrants.

THE DIGNITY OF IMMIGRANTS IN THE UNITED STATES

In the United States, some who do not welcome immigrants as a gift are worried about the "invasion" of illegal aliens, who allegedly steal jobs from citizens and take advantage of welfare systems. Harvard professor Samuel Huntington has lent his influential voice to these concerns. He predicted during the 1990s the coming "clash of civilizations." His book *Who Are We?* identifies forms of cultural conflict within the United States. Most notably, there are immigrants who do not assimilate to the values and customs of the dominant American culture, initially formed by English-speaking Protestants.

Huntington is especially worried about Hispanic immigrants, particularly Mexicans, who, in his opinion, are quite literally invading the United States. He complains that these immigrants represent a threat not only to "national security" but also to "societal security." He explains: "While national security is concerned, above all, with sovereignty, societal security is concerned above all with identity, the ability of a people to maintain their cultures, institutions, and way of life."[1] Huntington gives voice to the concerns of many people in the United States, concerns the Church cannot ignore in planning her mission. On the one hand, the Church must insist that each stranger is to be welcomed as a child of God and that cultural and racial differences can be gifts for everyone; on the other hand, the Church must help newly arrived immigrants offer their very distinctiveness as a gift to be shared rather than an obstacle that divides. This difference in approach was evident in the civil rights movement in the United States. One has only to note the contrast between the rhetoric of Reverend Dr. Martin Luther King, Jr., and that of the Black Power movement. Both sides in this pattern of tension must adjust in creating a peaceful society open to change in order to flourish.

Those who accept the presence of migrants but still believe they are not culturally and religiously equal to natives represent another serious challenge to the Church. The sense of superiority to immigrants is stronger in the receiving population when the immigrants come from poorer countries, as the majority of immigrants usually do. This is the challenge of class difference and racism, whose consequences are too quickly overlooked. Few have come to terms with these two powerful forces, which have been inherited from the past but are still very active within society and Church. The active power exercised by colonialism and racism within the Church is clear in words and attitudes that can convey the idea that "these people" are inferior. Who has not heard the usual complaints: they have no manners; their children are noisy; they do not financially support the parish; they are superstitious; they are poorly educated, or even illiterate; they need to be "evangelized"; and finally, they need to be "Americanized." The challenge is to bring all Catholics to accept wholeheartedly those of our faith—and others—who come from foreign countries, and to help them preserve and live their faith in this new country, their country of adoption. This process is multifaceted and mutual. Ideally, it enriches everyone; in fact, it is challenging to all. It makes clear, however, that the source of cultural disintegration is internal as well as external.

PASTORAL STRATEGIES

Summarizing these challenges under one heading, we could say that they represent the challenge of Catholicity. What do I mean by this? Simply that what we proclaim as a community of believers every Sunday, that we are a Catholic Church, is questioned day after day by the way in which we receive the migrants among us. Catholic migrants offer "the local Church the occasion to verify its Catholicity."[2]

Despite individuals such as criminals who are found in every group, at home and abroad, migrants are cultural treasures. Nations designate particularly significant objects as cultural treasures. Similarly, places are designated as heritage sites. In some cases, even persons gifted with exceptional abilities in an art or skill are designated as living national treasures. What the people, places, and objects so designated all have in common is that they help a culture to hand on from generation to generation what is most important in its roots and most precious among its treasures. The culture thus preserves its collective memory, expresses its unique identity and self-appreciation, and perpetuates itself. Migrants may be considered cultural treasures because they bring the riches of one culture into an encounter with another. Migrants enrich nations by promoting cultural exchange and interaction at very basic, neighborhood levels.

Migrants are also privileged protagonists of evangelization. Protagonists of evangelization take the Gospel into their own hearts and also call others to the conversion needed to live more fully as Christ wants all to live, as disciples who are members of his Body, the Church. Many Catholic migrants, although certainly not all, carry a vital faith in Christ, and they witness to him in their new country; in the host country, migrants call upon the generosity of the Catholics who receive them, thereby challenging native-born Catholics to live and proclaim the Gospel in a new way in their own country.

The migrant as a cultural treasure and as a privileged protagonist of the Gospel is acknowledged by members of the Church when we assert our Catholicity, that is, our radical openness to the cultural and religious "other," in our Church no less than in society. This openness becomes a reality when, following the example of the Lord, we recognize the faith and gift ·of the Roman centurion and the Canaanite woman of today (Mt 8:5–13; 15:21–28): the Mexican undocumented farmworkers; the Cuban and Haitian boat people; the Guatemalan housecleaners and nannies; the Chinese textile workers; the Sudanese refugees;

the Hmong and Vietnamese expatriates. It is once again Pope John Paul II who tells us: "Catholicity is not only expressed in the fraternal communion of the baptized, but also in the hospitality extended to the stranger, whatever his religious belief, in the rejection of all racial exclusion or discrimination, in the recognition of the personal dignity of every man and woman and, consequently, in the commitment to furthering their inalienable rights."[3] The Pope here expresses the crucial interreligious dimension of Catholicity and, we might add, strikes chords in harmony with what is best in the American tradition of welcoming immigrants, which all of our families once were on these shores.

In the United States, the challenge of Catholicity has to be worked out in terms of reconciling and uniting the "post-immigrant Church" to the "newly immigrant Church." The post-immigrant Church consists of the descendants of the "old immigrants," those who arrived in America during the nineteenth and early twentieth centuries. They represent the host society that too often gives the impression of having completely forgotten its immigrant heritage and the discrimination once suffered because of being Irish, German, Italian, Polish, Lithuanian, and Catholic. Descendants of these "old immigrants" are now very often the professionals and leaders at the center of American life and the Catholic Church. The newly immigrant Church comes less from Western Europe and more from Eastern Europe, Latin America, Africa, and Asia. In spite of their being "third worldly," or maybe because of it, these Latin American and African and Asian-Pacific Catholic "new immigrants" are helping to rejuvenate the U.S. Catholic Church and America itself.

Their inclusion in the normal life of the Church brings hope and bears promise for the future. The Church in the United States now has the potential of becoming sociologically universal in fact, of shaping a Catholic life that combines the heritage of the post-immigrant Church with the cultural gifts of the "new" immigrants. The "new" immigrants, when welcomed with respect, become agents of evangelization *ad intra* (within the Church herself) and *ad extra* (as a witness to God's Reign within society). They remind other Catholics of ways of faith that might have been forgotten, and their plight in society pulls other Catholics to work toward creating a society more just, charitable, and peaceful.

To address these challenges in the light of the vision given by faith, a number of pastoral initiatives would seem to be necessary in the Church and for the sake of the larger society. These responses are already in place but need to be further developed:

1. Everyone in the church must become more informed about the living situations of immigrants and those who receive them. The U.S. Catholic Bishops' decade-old campaign for immigration reform is designed to educate people about the more than 300,000 Catholics who have in recent years arrived annually in this country from all regions of the world. U.S. immigration laws and policies have lately become increasingly restrictive and have proven dangerous to some immigrants and asylum seekers. The separation of families and the suffering of children, the marginal lives of those who are in a country illegally, the less than human working conditions that cause great suffering have produced

thousands of stories that need to be better known. At the diocesan and parish levels, the Church attempts to foster an attitude of hospitality and welcoming among the host population. This step is very often taken for granted, ignoring the fact that some of our dioceses and parishes need explicit programs to help them learn to welcome newcomers. Many such programs are in place, but they need to be strengthened and expanded. Very often the welcome begins not with a parish but with an agency of Catholic Charities that offers immediate physical help and legal assistance. For their part, dioceses and the national bishops' conference welcome others by advocating for laws that respect their natural rights and dignity.

2.   Evangelization, conversion to the Gospel of Jesus Christ, must be at the center of all the Church's pastoral agendas and programs. The Church is "missionary by its very nature" (*Ad gentes* 2); without evangelization there is no Church. But evangelization has many dimensions: auto-evangelization (Paul VI said in *Evangelii nuntiandi* 15: "The Church is an evangelizer, but she begins by being evangelized herself"); primary evangelization (the mission to those who have yet to hear the Gospel for the first time); and reevangelization (re-presenting the faith to those who have abandoned it in practice and, sometimes, in theory). Welcoming immigrants to an evangelizing Church demands the kind of intense listening that distinguishes evangelization from proselytizing. It

means learning the language of the first generation in every wave of immigrants, even as they have to learn the language of their host country.

In order to be effective evangelizers, Catholics in the host culture have to allow themselves to be touched and shaped by Catholic immigrants' faith, values, and cultures. The role of popular religion is particularly important. What the "post-immigrant" U.S. Church has sometimes seen as "superstition" is the very medium that has kept, and still keeps, faith in God alive among new immigrants. In a more secularized and rationalist culture, popular religious devotions can be considered embarrassments, and some Catholics fully assimilated to American culture think them unnecessary at best. Popular devotions, however, carry the very heart of the culture and faith of a majority of Catholic immigrants today in the United States. An unwillingness by culturally established American Catholics to be changed by the immigrants and their popular religion is, along with the inadequate catechesis of Catholic immigrants themselves, one of the main reasons why immigrants leave the Catholic Church to join other religious groups.

3. The study of cultural dynamics and intercultural communication must become an essential component of formation within the Church, particularly in the seminaries, theological schools, and lay formation programs. We need to be trained to respect each other's cultures

and to deal forthrightly with cultural prejudices and generalizations. The effort to recognize God's influence in the *semina Verbi* (the seeds of the Word) in every culture can be a strong starting point for intercultural communication, in which host cultures and immigrant cultures enrich each other mutually by sharing their experiences of the Lord in his Church. Hampering this exchange are prejudices that have long histories and are quite hard to overcome. Prejudices will be attenuated only through developing personal relationships across cultural and racial boundaries and through a structured method for purifying historical and cultural memories. Programs that bring people together in a planned way for mutual conversation and prayer create a new dynamic in a Church open to all.

4. Youth ministry must be given special priority in pastoral agendas. The children of immigrants (the second generation) experience more than anybody else the conflict between tradition and national and global trends, between the host culture in which they have grown up and the immigrant culture of their parents. Some scholars and theologians have studied the condition of "in-betweenness" in which these young people live. How might this cultural in-betweenness become a treasure for the Church and a pastoral aid in the task of evangelization? Young people respond to peer ministry and help each other adjust to conditions their parents have not experienced. Attention to these spontaneous

adjustments will aid the Church's ministers in understanding how a parish or diocese might change to welcome everyone more successfully.

5. All these pastoral efforts will not work and will not last without a spirituality of Catholicity. To live from a Catholic vision is not just the fruit of our human effort. It is a gift from God and the result of profound and daily contemplation, of prayerful discernment in the cultural signs of the times of the gracious and always surprising presence of God. There cannot be mutual understanding and intercultural communication if "post-immigrants" and "new immigrants" fail to see God at work within cultural differences.

In this journey toward more authentic Catholicity, a journey that allows all to recognize the migrant as the bearer of cultural treasures and as a privileged protagonist of the Gospel, there will be tensions and conflicts, obstacles that seem insurmountable, and moments of desperation. The greatest social difficulty today, of course, is the illegal status of so many immigrants. A person's standing before the law determines how he or she is thought of by others, and the debate about how to resolve the status of the undocumented admits of no single clearly superior alternative. Nevertheless, none of these legal difficulties will destroy this necessary project of welcoming the immigrant if Catholics have cultivated a spirituality that has taught them that the mission is not theirs but God's, built on the vision of a truly Catholic Church that becomes the herald of a humanity celebrating the gifts of all cultures and enriched and given life by the seeds of the Gospel present in each of them.

At the close of the Second Vatican Council, Pope Paul VI declared that the spirituality of the Council was that of the Good Samaritan in the Gospel according to St. Luke (Luke 24). Jesus was responding to a challenge: Who is my neighbor? He explained that everyone in trouble is our neighbor and has claims on us. Faith gives us eyes to look at a stranger and see a neighbor, so that God will travel with both of us.

Economic Integration in the Hemisphere: The Continent of Hope

The subject of this chapter, which features very different evaluations of the capitalist system in North America and in South America, is something that has preoccupied me for many years. Conversations throughout our hemisphere have left me puzzled about how to formulate responses to both supporters and critics of the prevailing economic system. The social contract in the United States is implicitly predicated on a promise: if we accept economic inequality long enough, then, in the end, there will be more wealth for everyone. Each generation of Americans has expected to be better off economically than its predecessors. There is empirical evidence to support the promise's fulfillment in the history of the United States. As our national economy is no longer self-sufficient, however, increasing American wealth within the dynamics of a capitalist economic system means increasing trade with other nations and peoples. For the United States, this goal has meant removing national barriers to trade. For other countries in the Western Hemisphere, it has often meant preserving trade barriers that protect their fragile national economies from

U.S. competition. In the eyes of God and from the viewpoint of the poor, who is right?

Arguments for free trade between capitalist economies show how trade barriers prevent the creation of wealth. But there is also empirical evidence that free trade doesn't work for all and that the cost is too great for the poor of the world. We are confronted with moral ambiguity because it's hard to sort out facts marked by so many variables. We have to go forward, and we can't go forward so cautiously that we never speak clearly or take the small steps that will eventually make a great deal of difference. Nonetheless we go forward with the clear understanding that the whole economic order is not adequately understood by anybody and we have to keep searching together.

Globalization as an ideal, particularly in the economic order, is espoused in economic arguments that go back to Adam Smith (1723–1790) and David Ricardo (1772–1823), who pointed out that a free market for the exchange of consumer goods and services promotes the efficient use of production factors. The rewards structure of the market encourages efficiencies, including specialization, and redirects the efforts of less efficient producers to sectors more consistent with their resources and abilities. Ultimately, the argument goes, this efficiency means more plentiful and cheaper products for consumers. Additionally, a free market respects the preferences of those consumers, and, finally, the free market allows the prices of goods and services to reflect accurately the relationship of supply to demand, a relationship lost in a command economy. Assuming that developing states can find a market niche and can then fill it, and that tariff and nontariff trade barriers are removed, development will be promoted. If developing states are still too poor to enter the market, then multinational corporations can serve by expediting human and material capital transfers that eventually might allow the poorer countries to enter the global economy. And, finally, when dire economic needs are more visible, foreign aid is more likely to be delivered and, if well planned, contribute to the development of the country receiving the aid.

Economic arguments for ever freer trade have their counterparts in politics. First, permeable borders allow information inflow that can undermine authoritarian regimes and decrease the power of illegitimate nation-states. Second, rights abuses and famine and war—once they are visible worldwide because of global media attention—are more apt to be addressed for the benefit of the people. Third, connections between economics and international politics are affirmed. The promotion of liberal democracy through free trade and economic integration also protects human rights internally and promotes peace among nations.

Cultural arguments have their own importance in the debate about greater integration in the Western Hemisphere. When I was growing up, we never spoke about an American culture; we spoke about an American civilization. Other peoples had particular cultures. The immigrants had cultures: Mexican culture, Polish culture, Slovenian culture, Italian culture. We didn't have a culture; we had a civilization, an American order that was exemplary in its universal significance. In recent years we have become more self-reflective, and the cultural anthropologists now focus their scientific analyses on this country in a way they used to reserve for the "laboratories" of the South Sea Islands and tribal cultures. We have become aware that there is an American normative system—a particular culture—that teaches us how to think and what to do, what is important and what is not, and which is in competition with other equally important particular cultural systems. That development in cultural understanding is a step forward in Americans' recognizing their place and their proper contribution in a global order. The globalization of culture, sometimes mistakenly thought of as the world's assimilation to American culture, can truly foster human rights, can promote justice domestically and peace internationally, at least in theory.

But "globalization"—whether economic, political, or cultural—is an ambiguous and controversial term just because it comprises a simultaneous expansion and compression of time and space. On the one hand, globalization connects people and places around the world in a way not known earlier to the human race. On the other hand, those very connections have created a density of relationships that can become overwhelming and even oppressive to the human community. Many people want to escape, for a while at least, their place of work and their ordinary occupations; most of all, they want to escape their cell phones. These twin forces of expansion and compression create a powerful dynamic and reveal the deep contradictions within globalization, contributing to the fact that globalization draws both strong supporters and vehement detractors. The Church rejects slogans that make economic globalization either the source of all problems or their solution. We're back to a certain wariness in making moral judgments about an evangelically ambiguous phenomenon.

What might the Church contribute to a discussion about growth in trade and reduction in poverty in the context of globalization? The two principles of Catholic social teaching relevant to this discussion are solidarity and subsidiarity, working with the whole human family in mind while keeping decision making in local hands as much as possible. These terms are necessary because globalization, while it has its own logic, doesn't have its own ethic. The churches have to step forward, with the synagogues and the mosques, to bring ethical principles to bear on global economic activity.

The Catholic Church has a long history of addressing economics. Pope Leo XIII's encyclical *Rerum novarum* (1891), on the role of work and the rights of workers, began the Church's systematic reflection on the relationships among labor, capital, and social reconstruction. Leo XIII wrote at a moment, particularly in Italy, when the economy was moving from an agricultural to an industrial base. The Pope was most concerned about preserving the family. In an agricultural society organized as a subsistence economy, the family is an economic unit. Families work the fields together. As Italy became an industrialized nation and families moved from farms to cities, the father might work in a low-paying factory somewhere, and his wife might have to work as a domestic helper somewhere else. Often, the children were on their own. Sometimes the Church responded, as did St. John Bosco in nineteenth-century Italy. He gathered young boys who had been effectively abandoned by parents who had to work so hard that they could no longer care for their own children. Industrialization was destroying families, losing society's basic integrating factor. The Pope supported the idea not of an individual wage that was totally commensurate to the work done—"equal pay for equal work"—but of a *family wage*. The *family* and not the *individual* is the basis of the cultural and social order, Leo declared, and therefore should be the basis of the economic order.

Fast-forward to the twentieth century, as the relationships that now characterize globalization began to expand and intertwine, as economies became both wealthier and less self-sufficient, less national and more international. Pope John XXIII wrote in 1961: "One of the principal characteristics which seem to be typical of our age is an increase in social relationships . . . which have led to the introduction of many and varied forms of associations in the lives and activities of citizens."[1] Once again we see and experience an expansion and compression of relationships that create an extraordinary complexity.

As the human community continues to reorganize itself, the danger arises that human life and human community will be shattered in a way that will lead to alienation and therefore to social conflict. About twenty years ago, on the hundredth anniversary of Pope Leo XIII's encyclical on the dignity of work and workers, Pope John Paul II issued his own call to look at the "new things" of globalization that surround us, so that the world might embrace the future responsibly, proclaim the truth, and communicate the life that Christ has given us.[2]

An exclusive focus on economic factors as the measure of progress fails to penetrate to the heart of economic activity: the human person and the human community and, especially, the family. When the individual is considered apart from the bonds of family and culture and viewed primarily as a means of production or a source of consumption, completely fungible and entirely at the mercy of the vagaries of the market, we have at the center of our economy an artificial model. It does not correspond to who people truly are. The public logic of economic organization in our country is based on a sense of individualism that does not adequately correspond to human needs and personal dignity.

From an ethical perspective, then, the greatest danger of globalization is that our own terms of economic analysis will not serve in analyzing global complexities. It is not entirely unfair to say that, in this country, if you are between the ages of eighteen and thirty, not married, and in fine health, fairly smart, and have a good education, then the world is your oyster. But most people are not between the ages of eighteen and thirty and temporarily enjoying self-sufficiency—quite the opposite. So we have a social system that is largely designed with the lives of a very small minority of people in mind. Only incidentally do others get help as they scramble to find their way, sometimes with the help of government, sometimes with the help of companies and religious organizations, often relying on a generosity that is also part of the character of this country and that we can count on when the chips are really down. But the chips may have to get very far down before that generosity kicks in to provide the safety net necessary for an integrated society. If conceived on economic bases alone, society dissolves into a conglomeration of atomized individuals whose relationships with one another are characterized more by conflict than by cooperation or integration.

Public discourse about trade in a globalized world now permeates public debate. The terms of trade are set not by individuals but by government treaties. In the public debate, advocates of free trade point to the potential benefits for the countries sharing this hemisphere. The economist Paul Samuelson writes, "Free trade promotes a mutually profitable division of labor, greatly enhances the potential real national product of all nations, and makes possible higher standards of living all over the globe."[3]

Why, then, are there so many losers along with all the winners? Trade's creative capacity depends, in part, on its destructive tendency. Given its global reach, it is often difficult to fully
understand the compromises that trade forces upon all as jobs
are created or lost, as opportunities to enter the market and compete fairly seem open for some and not for others. When I was
growing up, the United States enjoyed a largely self-contained
economy. We exported oil and other raw materials. We consumed
our own produce and the goods we manufactured; there was
little dependence on external markets and no dependence on external debt. It is quite the opposite now. We are the most indebted
country in the world; without investment from China and other
nations that accept our money as their reserve currency, we would
be in much greater financial difficulties today. That we are now
a dependent economy becomes clear in a place like Chicago,
which was the quintessential industrialized city in the late nineteenth and early twentieth century, in a still national U.S. economy. The challenge is to find our way now in the global economy,
when our contribution is no longer primarily the manufactur-
ing component. Chicago has redesigned itself as a center for
financial services and has created a new commercial exchange in
the futures market.

In this evolving and complex situation, how does the Church
serve the evolving global order? The Church's voice is original in
every age. Just as the Lord himself was not understood very well by
the people of his own society, who tried to capture him in the categories that they inherited from their own historical experience, so
the Church's teaching is not grasped very easily by any society or
culture. Her voice is always original because in moral issues it is, in

fact, the voice of her Lord. Church people will inevitably be met with frequent misunderstanding. What the Church asks for after Vatican II is not privilege but simply the possibility of speaking freely and being heard.

In the last 120 years of the Church's "social teaching,"[4] the biblical call to care for the "least of these" has been well-developed in the international conferences sponsored by Latin American hierarchies. In the call of the poor, the Church hears an insistence that solidarity must be globalized. The voice of the Church in this hemisphere then speaks of trade and other aspects of globalization from the "bottom up." Decisions about particular applications are in the hands of governments and those elected for that purpose. Nonetheless, the Church's responsibility is to take part in the debate.

Our responsibility is to clarify moral principles and not ask first whose constituencies will be harmed and whose will be helped; not how you protect labor or how you permit more freedom for capital, but how we analyze who will be hurt and why. The very complexity and scope of contemporary economic activity and its extensive but anonymous impact on persons and communities make it incumbent upon lawmakers to ground public policy on sound ethical principles. I have found in speaking to members of the U.S. Congress that they have a sincere concern for the moral dimension of trade policy within our hemisphere. I was profoundly impressed by the moral seriousness with which they conducted their own business. Pastors of the Church should recognize that our moral concerns are shared by many in government. Sometimes the vocabulary is different and sometimes the decisions are ones that we cannot support; nonetheless, the moral concerns—because they are embedded in the human heart—are shared. In the analysis of those moral concerns and in the creation of an ethic that would be adequate to address the logic of globalization, the Catholic Church offers the two principles I mentioned at the beginning of this chapter: solidarity with all of humanity and subsidiarity in decision making.

These two principles underlie the analysis of economic activity given in *The Church in America* (*Ecclesia in America,* 1999). At its heart, genuine solidarity flows from an encounter with those whom we recognize as one with us, even with our differences. At its simplest, solidarity reminds us we are good samaritans to one another and therefore, in the words of Genesis, one another's keepers. Loving our neighbor clearly has universal dimensions in a globalized society. Universal solidarity fosters a way of acting in conformity with who we truly are, quite apart from political and economic logic; it teaches us to act in a way that will shape a world that is more free, more just, more charitable.

With its origins in God's own gracious communication of the divine life to his human creatures, solidarity is not just a vague notion of concern or even an explicit expression of mutual self-interest. Solidarity is a fundamental openness from the immediate world of one's own existence to situations and peoples in other places whom we may or may not know but whose actions and life are affected by ours. We are more than ever aware of interconnectedness in nature and in society. We witness the constructive nature of solidarity in the bonds on which life depends, in marriage and family, where the human tendency to be moved by concern for the other manifests itself. What moves us to act in solidarity is a belief in the sacred character and inherent dignity of human life. Such belief cannot be ignored, except at our own peril.

Against this natural drive to act in solidarity lies, however, the temptation to manipulate life, to turn life against life, to be indifferent to or destructive of the dignity of others and of all God's creation. This tendency, too, is evident in human relationships and can become embedded in unjust social structures at the national and global levels. Pope Paul VI's social teaching particularly addressed the question of unjust international economic structures. The Church recognizes the call in every age to overcome all forms of exploitation and oppression by grounding social cooperation in the dignity of each human person and the realities of human communities and traditions that tell us who we are. As Pope John Paul II said: "It is a question not only of alleviating the most serious and urgent needs through individual actions here and there, but of uncovering the roots of evil and proposing initiatives to make social, political and economic structures more just and fraternal."[5]

Complementary to solidarity with all of humanity is the notion of subsidiarity in decision making, a principle first elaborated by Pope Pius XI. Writing in the midst of the Great Depression, Pius XI developed the idea of a middle ground between laissez-faire capitalism on the one hand and various forms of collectivism, ideologies that subordinate the individual to the state, on the other. Instead of using individuals for its own all-inclusive purpose, the state should respect the role of "subordinate groups" within society and not usurp their rightful place as agents and organizing principles of human life.[6] This is the meaning of subsidiarity. It is a principle that fosters harmony among the different social groups that together constitute civil society as an organism, not as something that is planned and programmed from on high, or something that happens adventitiously, mechanistically from below, as if guided by an invisible hand. Subsidiarity respects the natural communities that, if they are related organically, will create a just and charitable civil society. Subsidiarity defines the rights and roles of states and other social institutions in ways that afford people their rightful place in making decisions that affect them and their communities.

Free trade advocates are sometimes critical of the Church's linking trade and social concerns. Some argue that trade agreements are clumsy vehicles for dealing with social questions such as workers' rights, environmental protection, or participation in decision making, especially in developing countries. These practical objections cannot be simply dismissed, but neither should they obscure the real linkages from the economy to social, political, and cultural life. In the Church's concern for an ethic of globalization, she has to make linkages between economic and other factors, and even introduce the social concerns into the negotiations around free trade.

Without an international effort to enforce decent labor conditions, workers run the risk of becoming rivals from country to country rather than cooperators in building a just social order globally. Workers in Central America will find themselves pitted against lower-paid workers in China and higher-paid—temporarily at least—workers in the United States. The reality of a so-called global commons where pollutants spill across national boundaries illustrates the need for regulation at the international level of all these issues. What the regulation turns out to be and what is to be the regulatory agency are technical questions that the Church cannot address with any expertise. What the Church has to address is the *need* to address them.

Fair trade between countries is an instrument for achieving greater economic integration; the gains of increased trade need to be complemented by domestic policy reforms that distribute these benefits equitably. Here, the dynamics of cultural analysis and theological reflection can contribute. Very often an economic model might be good within proper legal and cultural frameworks, but, if these frameworks are weak or deficient because the juridical and legal orders are not well-established in a country and because the local culture itself is not based on human solidarity, free trade agreements can inflict great injustice on the poor. No matter what kind of international trade agreements might be reached, they will not foster genuine human development if the local culture countenances a corruption that keeps the rich in control and the poor without voice.

It is arguable that the liberalized market model the United States holds up for the rest of the world to imitate is only half of our own reality. We don't speak often enough about the other part of our society, our concern for social safety nets. We have a long tradition of unemployment benefits and protections that give workers important support in times of great difficulty. America is, in fact, a mixture of free market ideals and social welfare realities. If we are to offer a model to others in our hemisphere, we should offer both sides of who we are and how our system truly operates.

The developing horizon of economic cooperation must include means of securing morally just development and authentic freedom for all. We should assure development by living more self-consciously in solidarity with people who are not our co-citizens but who inhabit this hemisphere now experiencing new forms of integration. Behind the promise of economic integration stands God's promise of a world where the poor inherit the earth and peacemakers are blessed (Mt 5:3–10). This is the constant in every human project that supports our conviction that, with God's help and guidance, America can be truly the continent of hope.

Reconsidering National Sovereignty: Is God at Work in Globalization?

God is at work where charity and self-sacrifice and forgiveness unite people who would otherwise be separated, where good consequences overcome evil actions, where hope remains constant in the midst of despair, where new life comes from death. How is God active in the experience of globalization, of relativizing the barriers separating people as citizens of different nation-states? This topic must be approached with awareness of the fact that any vision of globalization is seen from each one's historical perspective, with an eye toward a sketchily visualized future. Inevitably, of course, each of us speaks also from personal experience. I find myself discerning the future as a bishop of the Catholic Church, responsible for a universal church's life and ministries in Illinois's Cook and Lake counties. I come to this role and to this topic as a member of a worldwide missionary religious congregation, one that has brought me into some extended personal contact with very poor people on every continent. I come also as a cardinal priest of the city of Rome. Rome was the capital of an empire with universal pretensions when the Catholic Church was born in one of its more unruly provinces two thousand years ago. I am a citizen of the United States of America, a country that sometimes claims ancient Rome's universal prerogatives. Our country's political and economic role in the emerging global society is shifting because of the economic growth of China, India, and Latin America. Within the United States, as in other countries, the Church can be, at times, a locus for God's activity and sometimes, therefore, unsettling in its activities, because God is not a citizen of any nation-state. I mention all this because it is part of the perspective that necessarily informs much of what follows and will become explicit in a few concluding observations.

The Catholic convert G. K. Chesterton once quipped that the search for extraterrestrial intelligence will prove successful when the future space explorer lands on a planet and discovers a tablet inscribed with the injunction "Thou shalt not kill." Chesterton's point was that, along with other irrefutable signs of intelligence—knowledge of mathematics, invention of cities, social organization, and so on—an alien civilization will inevitably recognize the inherent dignity of its own intelligent minds; and such recognition will occur when they see that their claim on the nonviolent behavior of their neighbors, their fellow intelligences, must be inviolable.

To explain why this topic of globalization and national sovereignty must once again begin with a reflection on truth and its relation to human reason and historical religion, let me cite an intriguing passage from Daniel Dennett's philosophical meditation on Darwinian theory, *Darwin's Dangerous Idea:*

> Suppose SETI [the Search for Extra-Terrestrial Intelligence] struck it rich, and established communication with intelligent beings on another planet. We would not be surprised to find that they understood and used the same arithmetic that we do. Why not? Because arithmetic is *right*. . . . The point is clearly not restricted to arithmetic, but to all "necessary truths"—what philosophers since Plato have called *a priori* knowledge.[1]

Similarly, we may expect to find a commandment against murder both on earth and on that still undiscovered planet, because the natural moral law is not just *right* but part of what it means to be intelligent. Intelligence, in other words, that can recognize mathematical truths and the laws of nature that govern phenomena such as gravity will also inevitably recognize the natural moral law that says intelligence possesses an inherent dignity whose right to its own life and that same right on the part of other intelligences may not be violated.

Chesterton's anecdote helps elucidate one basis of creaturely unity and points to God's activity in uniting again the human race he created as one on this planet. Human reason has always recognized the evil of murder and the benefits of a peaceful society based on that recognition of primordial unity. The condemnation of murder is hardly unique to the Ten Commandments of Mount Sinai. So what role does a religion that searches for signs of God's influence in temporal events play in this universal rational recognition of moral truth? Chesterton's thought experiment suggests that a belief in God is not necessarily entailed in a recognition of the truths of mathematics or even the moral law, although elsewhere he suggests—in common with the Platonic tradition in philosophy—that the recognition of a priori truths and the natural moral law also entails at least some form of philosophical theism.

Even Europe's most famous and influential atheist, Friedrich Nietzsche, recognized the connection between the search for universal truth and the presence of divinity in the world. In *The Gay Science,* his conscious mockery of the good news, Nietzsche wrote, "It is still a metaphysical faith upon which our faith in science rests . . . even we knowers of today, we godless antimetaphysicians, still take *our* fire, too, from the flame lit by the thousand-year-old faith, the Christian faith which was also Plato's faith, that God is the truth; that truth is divine."[2]

Forgetful of Nietzsche's insights, Richard Dawkins opens his book *The God Delusion* with this depiction of the utopia that awaits us, if only we would cast off the security blanket of religion:

> Imagine, with John Lennon, a world with no religion. Imagine no suicide bombers, no 9/11, no 7/7, no Crusades, no witch-hunts, no Gunpowder Plot, no Indian partition, no Israeli/Palestinian wars, no Serb/Croat/Muslim massacres, no persecution of Jews as "Christ-killers," no Northern Ireland "troubles," no "honor killings," no shiny-suited bouffant-haired televangelists fleecing gullible people of their money ("God wants you to give till it hurts"). Imagine no Taliban to blow up ancient statues, no public beheadings of blasphemers, no flogging of female skin for the crime of showing an inch of it.[3]

Here again Nietzsche, the great nineteenth-century pro-claimer that "God is dead," blocks the way to such lazy utopias, for *his* atheism at least is honest enough to admit that a denial of God entails a world of violence. As R. J. Hollingdale says in his biography, *Nietzsche: The Man and His Philosophy,* "Nineteenth-century rationalism was characterized by insight into the diffi-culty in accepting revealed religion, and obtuseness regarding the consequences of rejecting it."[4] Ignoring the bloody history of Dawkins's own country's colonialism and imperialism, we need only look at the history of the United States and see that every generation has had its war, whether fought in the name of national independence or manifest destiny, whether genocide against the indigenous peoples, whether rooted in racial slavery or in economic dominance, whether undertaken for the defense of democracy or the advance of freedom. The history of orga-nized American violence has been uncaused and uncontrolled by religion. Dawkins's historical tale is hypocritical.

Nietzsche himself seemed to foresee the violence of the twen-tieth century in one of his last books, his autobiography, *Ecce Homo,* where he spoke in the cadences of an unbelieving Jere-miah: "Shocks are bound to ensue, and a spell of earthquakes such as the world has never yet imagined even in its dreams. The concept 'politics' then becomes elevated entirely to the sphere of spiritual warfare. All the mighty realms of the ancient order of society are blown into space—for they are all based on falsehood: there will be wars, the like of which have never been seen on earth before. Only from my time and after me will poli-tics on a large scale exist on earth."[5]

The record of the twentieth century, which has continued

into the present century, remains in the background of our reflections: there is great variety in world religions, and that variety has sometimes had lethal consequences, even in global society today. But if we grant Nietzsche's point that faith and reason cannot be divorced without the separation carrying its own lethal consequences, we must ask how both reason and religion in cooperation can contribute to the search for truths that ground or at least give hope for peace in a truly global society.

If both reason and religion make truth claims that are universal, then it seems obvious to both Chesterton and Nietzsche, if not to Dawkins, that, when reason and religion are separated, each will foster violence. When united in ways that respect all claims, reason and religion open paths to universal peace, as long as the world is so arranged that both faith and reason are allowed their proper spheres of competence. A reason closed in on itself will create rationalist utopias where every moral depravity can be justified, as the great totalitarian systems of the twentieth century, founded on so-called scientific principles, amply proved. When human autonomy becomes the only ethical imperative in a society intentionally constructed to function as if God did not exist (*etsi Deus non daretur*),[6] violence ineluctably becomes a necessary element, as Marx insisted, in reaching allegedly rational forms of political society. Far more people have been subjected to violence and death not only for rationalist utopias but even in the name of justice, freedom, democracy, and national independence, as recalled earlier, than were ever killed in the wars of religion.

Yet we should humbly acknowledge there has been violence in the name of religion, and different religions see differently the relationship of reason to revelation and faith. If every reli-

gion admitted that God does not approve of the killing of inno-
cents, then the religious motivation for violence would disappear.
But the headlines teach us differently. So how can this problem
be honestly addressed?

The first point to make is that the word "religion" is highly
ambiguous. People belong not to religion but only to *a* religion,
just as human beings speak not language but *a* language and are
related politically to *a* nation-state. Thus one cannot speak of religion as a bulwark for unity, peace, or freedom in any social
context without specifying *which* religion is being discussed. I
am, of course, most qualified to speak of Catholicism, which, as
explained in Chapter 6, has a long history of morally justifying
warfare in certain restricted circumstances and of upholding
the value of peace at all times. The Church returned again to the
relation between faith and reason and their relation to violence
in Pope Benedict XVI's controversial 2006 address at the University of Regensburg in Germany. This speech was devoted to
discussing the relationships between religion and reason in
secularist societies and only tangentially to the role of reason in
Islamic theology. The Pope spoke of unacceptable trends in late
medieval Catholic theology that divorced faith from reason, over-
emphasized the role of human will, and weakened both Catholic
theology and European civilization with effects harmful to
this day. But the Catholic Church eventually came to a definitive
stance regarding the relation between faith and reason in the
First Vatican Council's 1870 decree *Dei filius*, which solemnly
declared that reason, properly used, will lead to a recognition of
God's existence. Critics of that decision pointed to the irony that
Catholics were now obligated by their faith to believe in the power
of reason. But the irony belongs to the scoffers, as Chesterton

pointed out: oftentimes the purpose of authority in religion is to rescue reason for the world.

By definition, however, historical religions make claims that reach beyond reason to a divine revelation. What happens when, to quote Blaise Pascal, "reason's final step is to recognize that there is an infinity of things beyond it"?[7] The word "revelation" means a lifting or a pulling back of some veil to display truths that would otherwise be inaccessible. In terms of the phenomenology of religion, revelation occurs because of God's initiative; it is always understood that God is the one who is retracting the curtain, revealing truths "hidden before the foundations of the world" (Ps 78:2). The question then becomes: To what extent does revelation supersede, abolish, or confirm truths of reason that seem to place constraints on human freedom? Throughout the centuries, various religions and schools of theology have given different answers.

The Catholic consensus would be that—besides revealing truths otherwise inaccessible to reason (the Resurrection of Christ, for example)—revelation confirms the truths of the natural moral law, and does so by giving them a higher grounding. As Pope Benedict XVI said in his first encyclical, *Deus caritas est* (*God Is Love,* 2005): "In a world where the name of God is sometimes associated with vengeance or even a duty of hatred and violence, this message [the revelation of God as love] is both timely and significant."[8] It also sets in intellectual perspective the constant human pursuit of freedom, freedom to search for and hold to the truth of things in public discussion and freedom to love God and neighbor in public expression.

Benedict XVI had a chance to explain that same message

during his African pilgrimage when, on March 19, 2009, he spoke to twenty-two Muslim leaders who met him in Yaoundé, Cameroon. "Genuine religion widens the horizon of human understanding and stands at the base of any authentically human culture," the Pope said. "It rejects all forms of violence and totalitarianism, not only on principles of faith, but also of right reason. Indeed, religion and reason mutually reinforce one another, since religion is purified and structured by reason, and reason's full potential is unleashed by revelation and faith." In other words, both reason and faith are corrupted when not in constant dialogue with each other.

John Allen, the Rome correspondent for the *National Catholic Reporter*, was on assignment with the papal party and interviewed Sheikh Mohama Oussani Waziri, a highly regarded imam in his country, shortly after the Pope's address. When Allen asked Sheikh Waziri whether he agreed with the Pope's remark that "genuine religion . . . rejects all forms of violence and totalitarianism," the sheikh responded: "All mainstream figures are in agreement on that, though there's a small minority that rejects it. Every religious tradition has its extremists, who tend to exploit fear and thus encourage divisions—both within their own tradition, and between traditions." Then, when Allen asked about the recent flash point in Nigeria, during the attempt to impose Shariah (Islamic law) in the northern provinces of that country, this Islamic cleric replied: "As a theological matter, Shariah, in the sense in which you're describing it, doesn't exist. I speak now as someone who has studied Islamic law in Egypt and Syria, working on a Ph.D. in the subject. In Islamic teaching, Shariah can never be imposed. Accepting it has to be an act of your own will. The Qur'an is very clear on this point: there must be no obligation in Islam."[9]

While Sheikh Waziri is only one voice among many in African Islam, his remarks make it clear that a conversation is taking place, a rational conversation using religion to discredit violence and protect human freedom. How much these modest shoots of dialogue will lead to global peace is still unknown. But at least this can be said: Pope Benedict's powerful pilgrimage to Africa is itself a good example of the role the papacy has increasingly taken on as an advocate of peace. This work involves relativizing the absolute claims of nation-states upon their citizens' behavior.

In the face of religiously motivated violence, we often forget how the history of violence in the last four hundred years is bound up with the creation of the modern nation-state, and we often assume that reason is *universal,* and therefore is the basis of human unity, whereas faith is *particular,* completely determined by the specific religion one has faith in, and therefore a source of discord. Catholicism argues to the contrary, that faith is universal and that, in an era of nationalist violence, religion is called to protect the legitimacy of reason and of the various religious cultures that antedate restrictive nationalisms.

Of course, for faith to assume this culture-protecting role, the diverse religions of the world must recognize both reason and the moral law that is based on the inherent and innate rationality of the human person as such. Second, if the religions of the world are to serve as the guardians of human culture and human freedom, they must do so by grounding each culture in the universal natural moral law. That was the foundation of Vatican II's teaching both on religious liberty and on interreligious dialogue. The Church could never have reaffirmed the primacy of personal conscience except on the basis of her affirmation of the common natural moral law; nor could Vatican II have affirmed the goodness present in each religion except on the basis of the dignity of every human person. Every particularity is related to the whole, every specificity is a concrete instance of what is universal.

This conviction about the basis for the inviolability of conscience and for the Church's appreciation of other religions is grounded not in something new but in her own acceptance of the truth of the revelation she believes the world has received from God in Jesus Christ. In other words, preaching the Gospel of Christ and affirming the goodness present in other religions go hand in hand. Here is how Pope John Paul II put the matter in an important speech to various leaders of world religions in Los Angeles in 1987:

> Throughout my Pontificate it has been my constant concern to fulfill this twofold task of proclamation and dialogue. On my pastoral visits around the world I have sought to encourage and strengthen the faith of Catholic people and other Christians as well. At the same time, I have been pleased to meet leaders of all religions in the hope of promoting greater inter-religious understanding and cooperation for the good and the peace of the human family.[10]

John Paul II then addressed the Buddhist community, the Islamic community, the Hindu community, the Jewish community, speaking to each in terms they could recognize as their own. This was a conversation that would have been impossible without the conviction that reason is universal and that different religions can use reason and their own sense of revelation to reach across racial, national, cultural, ideological, and even religious differences in order to foster a dialogue that creates relationships that will encourage peace and promote freedom. What is fascinating about John Paul's address is that he sees his task as not just strengthening the faith of Catholics but also to bring out the best in all the religions of the world.

How was he able to accomplish that seemingly impossible task? He could do so because of his conviction that faith and reason complement each other. This means that just as reason is universal, so is faith, precisely because truth is universal. As he puts it in *Fides et ratio:* "The word of God is not addressed exclusively to any one people or to any one period of history. Similarly, dogmatic statements, while reflecting at times the culture of the period in which they were defined, formulate an unchanging and ultimate truth."[11] One part of that universal truth is that all religions, without exception, share in some mysterious way in the truth. There is a dynamic in the act of faith itself that brings new discoveries and unfolds new insights and developments consonant with the way reason by its nature searches constantly for truth, while rejoicing in the appreciation of truths already discovered. To quote John Paul II once more: "To believe it possible to know a universally valid truth is in no way to encourage intolerance; on the contrary, it is the essential condition for sincere and authentic dialogue between persons. On this basis alone is it possible to overcome divisions and to journey together towards full truth, walking those paths known only to the Spirit of the Risen Lord."[12]

With this insight, we see how the real threat to world peace comes not from "religion" considered as some abstract entity but from the loss of meaning that inevitably follows from the divorce of faith and reason. To quote Pope John Paul II one last time:

> One of the most significant aspects of our current situation . . . is "the crisis of meaning." Perspectives on life and the world, often of a scientific temper, have so proliferated that we face an increasing fragmentation of knowledge. This makes the search for meaning difficult and often fruitless. Indeed, still more dramatically, in this maelstrom of data and facts in which we live and which seem to comprise the very fabric of life, many people wonder whether it still makes sense to ask about anything. The array of theories, which vie to give an answer, and the different ways of viewing and of interpreting the world and human life, serve only to aggravate this radical doubt, which can easily lead to skepticism, indifference or to various forms of nihilism.
>
> In consequence, the human spirit is often invaded by a kind of ambiguous thinking which leads it to an ever deepening introversion, locked within the confines of its own immanence without reference of any kind to the transcendent. A philosophy which no longer asks the question of the meaning of life would be in grave danger of reducing reason to merely accessory functions, with no real passion for the search for truth.[13]

Faith and reason are universal because truth is universal. Moreover, truth from every source sets us free. It liberates us to discern
good from evil, and therefore to see what is good in all religions,
insofar as they participate in the truth, and what is evil in them,
which surfaces when some among them sanction violations of
the natural moral law. But these violations are precisely that: violations, as the etymological link between "violence" and "violation" already makes clear. St. Paul says,

> When Gentiles who have not the law do by nature what
> the law requires, they are a law to themselves, even though
> they do not have the law. They show that what the law
> requires is written on their hearts, while their conscience
> also bears witness and their conflicting thoughts accuse
> or perhaps excuse them on that day when, according to
> my gospel, God judges the secrets of men by Christ Jesus
> (Rom 2:14–16).

If we are not convinced that reason and faith together can
attain truth, then every dialogue or conversation about any aspect of human experience degenerates into a negotiation about
often opposing interests, whether personal or social. And when
such negotiations fail, as they inevitably do, violence follows, and
peoples lose their freedom.

All this leads to a more practical question: Where in the
world do we find institutionalized the relationships necessary to
foster the universalism that gives hope for permanent peace and
the safeguarding of personal freedom? We speak of a global
economy, global political and cultural trends, global means of
communication, and global technologies. Each of these is sup-

ported by many institutions, none with complete global reach. We know their inadequacy because we have experienced a conversion of imagination in our lifetime, inspired by that magnificent photo of the earth taken during the 1969 *Apollo 8* mission to the moon, a snapshot of a globe beautiful but fragile floating in an infinite sea of darkened space: our planet, home to all of us. Ecological consciousness has inspired in recent decades a global movement to reconsider all human activities in the light of their impact on the entire earth. But will this, like the universalism of the Enlightenment or the worldwide communist movement, become one more ideology, sure to claim its share of victims among the earth's inhabitants?

First of all, as we identify ourselves as inhabitants of the globe, no particular nation-state can be an adequate international base for the universal network of relationships in which we find ourselves and in which we hope to establish peace securely. We like to read American history as an experiment in a universal quest for freedom, and this is in part true; but others do not always see us in this light, even when they appreciate our often good efforts and still condemn the mistakes we have made and continue to make in the name of our self-proclaimed exceptionalism. I have visited with very poor people around the globe as part of a missionary congregation, whose life and ministry I guided and encouraged for many years. Everywhere, even in Marxist countries, people knew who I was as a Catholic priest. They might not have agreed with or might even have entirely opposed what I stood for, but I was an acknowledged part of their life in some sense. If I was distrusted, it wasn't because I was a priest, a man with a universal identity, but because I was an American, a citizen of a powerful but particular nation. A personal anecdote will illustrate the point.

In the 1970s, I was in and out of Zaire, the former Belgian Congo in Central Africa. Ruled then by President Mobutu, it was a country with little medicine because the minister of health had taken the money for medical supplies to advance the cause of his own tribe. In the interior villages of what is now again called the Congo, if there was any medical help at all, it came from two sources: a clinic run by Catholic religious sisters and a clinic organized by USAID. From the sisters, who had ways to bring medicine into the country without going through regular government channels, one could get aspirin and vitamins and perhaps some penicillin. From the U.S. clinic, one could get only condoms. The Congolese asked me: "Why does your government hate us? What is your government telling us when they give us gifts to stop us from having children? Our children are our wealth, our future." A state that does not bother to consult the people it purports to help before showing up with "aid" will always be regarded with suspicion, no matter what its own intention may be.

In a global society, it is more sectarian to be French or Chinese or American than to be Christian, Muslim, or Buddhist. The great cultures of the world have been created in dialogue with the great religious faiths, and the faiths will be the major carriers of culture and of a deeper source of personal identity in a globalized society than will be the nation-states now evolving into different forms of "sovereignty."

When Pope Benedict XVI visited the United States in 2008, he spoke to the General Assembly of the United Nations and called those representing the world's governments to think beyond nationalisms and their various interests to what is demanded of us by reason of our participating in a common human family.

He spoke of the violation of universal human rights by particular governments and challenged the UN to find nonviolent and collective ways to rescue citizens of nations from the oppression of their own governments. This is a vision of universalism, of globalism, challenging an organization created by nation-states in order to diplomatically negotiate peace among themselves to evolve into a forum for the protection of the entire human family from the violence of those very founding nation-states, sometimes against their own citizens. The speech respected the two poles of Catholic social teaching: subsidiarity, let decisions be made as much as possible where they will be carried out; and solidarity, let decisions be made keeping in mind the whole network of relationships that bind us together as human beings.

When Pope Paul VI spoke before the General Assembly of the United Nations in the visit mentioned in Chapter 5, he explained that he came without political or economic power of any sort; he came, he said, as "an expert in humanity." He could make that claim on the basis of the rational and doctrinal universalism discussed earlier and with the memory of two thousand years of living with and accompanying the human family around the world, in good times and in bad. In the name of the human race, he appealed to the leaders of the nations to eschew all violence, all war: *"Jamais plus la guerre!"* (War never again!) To give up the right to make war independently is, of course, in the political order we have inherited, to give up part of a nation's claim to sovereignty. The Pope knew who he was and what he was asking. Before the entire world, gathered as separate nation-states, the Holy Father alone was in his own home.

Paul VI's predecessor, Pope John XXIII, called the Second

Vatican Council fifty years ago because he had lived through the violence of the first half of the twentieth century. He had seen nations destroy each other over their sovereign rights in the First World War. He had seen classes turn on one another in the Communist revolutions. He had seen racial and cultural hatreds justify the genocide of the Jews and the slaughter of the Slavic peoples. He had seen how colonial empires oppressed peoples and how economic advantage subsumed concern for workers themselves. He asked who would tell the peoples of the world that they are brothers and sisters. He wrote his letter to all peoples on peace, and he hoped that the Catholic Church could be an agent in establishing a more permanently peaceful world. He called a council that began to strengthen networks of relationships among Christians; among peoples of other faiths, also seekers of truth; and among people of no faith, who are in their own way also seekers. Among those working for justice and for universal peace and freedom, he asked for greater cooperation. In that council, the Church defined herself as the living sign, the sacrament, of the unity of the human race. As John XXIII and his successors have acknowledged, Catholics have often failed to be God's instruments in creating unity, but God's work is greater than ours and his power overcomes, throughout history, our weakness and sinfulness.

The Catholic Church at her best, along with other universal religions, is always a distinctive voice in every society, neither co-opted nor isolated, although some will try to do one or the other, to make religion a Department of State or else to set it aside in such a way that it has no public influence. Perhaps more than through any program or plan, religion advances peace by assuring the world that forgiveness, even of one's enemies, is possible, because God wants to forgive and gives us the power to do so. Without the God-given power to forgive, no one can be truly free. The travails of human freedom have been traced from its birth in God's creating man and woman, its external constraints in positive law, its demands in intrinsic natural law, and its safeguard in revealed truths that are rationally defensible if admitted to public discourse. Freedom will flourish in a more globalized society if the world's ethics reflect this natural moral law.

Let me conclude by recalling another event that provides an image of God's unifying action in the world. At the funeral of Pope John Paul II, the whole world—political leaders, religious representatives, and people, especially young people—assembled in St. Peter's Square in Rome. They were there not to deliberate or to dialogue or to decide, not to fight or to make money, not to compete in any way, or to be entertained. They were there to honor a peacemaker who knew who he was and in what he was rooted, and whose love was bigger than the globe itself. Together, freely and reasonably, we worshiped the God of peace to whom Pope John Paul II had totally given himself. God himself, the giver of faith and the author of reason, was forging a new unity among his human creatures. The promise of globalization was glimpsed in a memorable but fleeting occasion that demonstrated the bases of ecclesial communion and human solidarity.

Postscript

Utopias and the Kingdom of God

In the summer of 2010, at the invitation of the archbishop of Morelia, I visited the Mexican state of Michoacán, from where many of the Catholics in the Archdiocese of Chicago have migrated. Michoacán's history is bound up with the story of Vasco de Quiroga, its founding bishop. He was a lawyer, a humanist, a friend of Thomas More in a European society still unified by Catholicism before the advent of the modern nation-state and its initial religious justification in the Protestant Reformation. Don Vasco saw that the clash between Spanish rule and the way of life of the indigenous peoples of Mexico could be resolved by giving a Catholic religious basis to their authentically communal lifestyle. He helped the P'urhépecha people create a fair society, building on their traditions read in the light of Thomas More's *Utopia,* integrating health care, agricultural development, and craft production; creating a model for education at all levels; relying on the native tradition of community hospitality and the people's sense of fairness and justice. He remains, even today, the *"tata,"* the father of Michoacán society.

The state of Michoacán, like every human society, is not the Kingdom of God. Throughout human history, however, various utopian schemes have been proposed, because the status quo in every age is always less than what human beings aspire toward. Utopias are not usually blueprints for present action so much as pictures of what human society and the cosmos might become, if God were free to act and if everything conformed to his purposes. Utopian literature most often extrapolates from our hopes; it eventually fails when used prescriptively, because human community trips up over human sinfulness. The people determine the relative success or failure of the idea. The nineteenth-century Transcendentalist movement in America encouraged communal life separated from ordinary society for the sake of transcendent ideals. Its noble experiments failed, their adherents dispersed, but they served to remind a newly industrializing and materialist society that human activity has a transcendent goal.

Much of this book has argued that the legacy of Enlightenment social theory and its economic and political thought has mistakenly relegated religion to the private sphere and tried to solve the problems of public order by directing the power of the sovereign state in accord with "secular" reasons, ignoring the action of God. Whether governed by social theories that address contemporary problems or by utopian schemes that bring us to alternative communities beyond contemporary problems, human activity left to its own resources inevitably fails.[1] The Church's mission, by contrast, is to proclaim hope in every situation and to prepare people to live in the Kingdom of God.

The last book of the New Testament, the Apocalypse or the Revelation to John, makes no attempt to portray human activity or to justify it rationally. The Apocalypse reveals the human race waiting for God, watching God in action as he creates a new heaven and a new earth. It is God who "makes all things new," because only God can create something from nothing. God does not rearrange the furniture of the present social and economic and political orders; he provides the very being of a human race that deserves respect in all circumstances but enjoys eternal life only when transformed by God's grace. In every age and every place, the most important human activity is to watch for God's.

NOTES

INTRODUCTION

1. Friedrich Schleiermacher, *On Religion: Speeches to Its Cultured Despisers* (Cambridge: Cambridge University Press, 1996), 23.
2. *The Christian Faith* (Edinburgh: T&T Clark, 1989), 12ff.
3. Borrowing the term from his friend, Romain Rolland. See Sigmund Freud, *Civilization and Its Discontents* (New York: Norton, 1961), 11.

CHAPTER 1

1. Alexis de Tocqueville, *Democracy in America* (New York: Harper and Row, 1969), 430.
2. Interview with Nathan Gardels, published in Leszek Kolakowski, *My Correct Views on Everything* (South Bend, Ind.: St. Augustine Press, 2005), and reprinted in *New Perspectives Quarterly* 26, no. 4/27, no. 1.
3. Joseph Cardinal Ratzinger (Pope Benedict XVI), *Values in a Time of Upheaval* (San Francisco: St. Ignatius Press, 2006), 29.
4. See Appendix, Matthew Spalding and Patrick J. Garrity, *A Sacred Union of Citizens* (Lanham, Mass.: Rowman & Littlefield, 1996), 175 ff.
5. Query XVIII, *The Portable Jefferson* (New York: Penguin, 1976), 215.
6. Response to a question posed by John Brockman, "God (or Not), Physics and, of Course, Love: Scientists Take a Leap" in the *New York Times*, January 4, 2005.

CHAPTER 2

1. *Lemon v. Kurtzman,* 403 U.S. 602 at 622 (1971).
2. *Lee v. Weisman,* 505 U.S. 577 at 595 (1992).
3. Second Vatican Council, *Dignitatis Humanae [Declaration on Religious Liberty]* 1 (1965).
4. Lee J. Strang, "The Meaning of 'Religion' in the First Amendment," *Duquesne Law Review* 40 (Winter 2002): 181.
5. *School District of Grand Rapids v. Ball,* 473 U.S. 373, 385 (1985).
6. *McCollum v. Board of Education,* 333 U.S. 203 (1948).
7. *McCollum v. Board of Education,* 333 U.S. 203 at 228 (1948).
8. *Lynch v. Donnelly,* 465 U.S. 668 (1984).
9. *County of Allegheny v. ACLU,* 492 U.S. 573 at 595, footnote 46 (1989).
10. *Locke v. Davey,* 540 U.S. 712 (2004).
11. *U.S. v. DeJesus,* 347 F.3d 500 at 510 (3rd Cir. 2003).

CHAPTER 3

1. Oliver Wendell Holmes, "The Path of the Law," *Harvard Law Review* 10 (1897): 469.
2. Ibid., 461.
3. *Planned Parenthood v. Casey,* 505 U.S. 833 at 856 (1992).
4. Ibid.
5. Joseph Raz, *The Morality of Freedom* (Oxford: Clarendon Press, 1986), 162.
6. *Maynard v. Hill,* 125 U.S. 190 (1888).
7. *Pierce v. Society of Sisters,* 268 U.S. 190 at 211 (1888).
8. Concurring opinion, *Griswold v. Connecticut,* 381 U.S. 479 at 486 (1965).
9. Dissenting opinion, *Estin v. Estin,* 334 U.S. 541 (1948).
10. Dissenting opinion, *Poe v. Ullman,* 367 U.S. 497 (1961).
11. J. Finnis, "Natural Law: The Classical Theory," in J. Coleman and S. Shapiro, eds., *Oxford Handbook on Jurisprudence and Legal Philosophy* (Oxford: Oxford University Press, 2001).

CHAPTER 4

1. Henry de Lubac, *At the Service of the Church* (San Francisco: Ignatius, 1993), 171–72.

2. Peter Singer, *Practical Ethics* (Cambridge: Cambridge University Press, 1993), 87.

CHAPTER 5

1. John Paul II, Address to the Pontifical Academy for Life, February 24, 1998.

2. Fred Dings, "Letter to Genetically Engineered Superhumans," in *Eulogy for a Private Man* (Evanston, Ill.: TriQuarterly Books/Northwestern University Press, 1999), 25.

CHAPTER 6

1. St. Augustine, *The City of God*, XIX, 13 (Cambridge: Cambridge University Press, 1998), 938.

2. Gregory of Nyssa, "On Perfection," *The Greek Orthodox Theological Review* 29, no. 4 (1984): 349–79.

3. Catechism of the Catholic Church, 2nd edition (New York: Doubleday, 1995), 2304.

4. Address to the General Assembly of the United Nations, April 18, 2008.

5. Message of John Paul II, World Day of Peace, January 1, 2002.

6. Benedict XVI, Address to the Roman Curia and Papal Representatives, December 21, 2009.

CHAPTER 7

1. Russell Shorto, "With God at Our Desks: The Rise of Religion and Evangelism in the American Workplace," *New York Times Magazine,* October 31, 2004, 42.

2. Anne Fremantle, ed., *A Treasury of Early Christianity* (Fort Collins, Colo.: Roman Catholic Books, 1953), 42–43.

3. "We Aren't Whining, We Do Work Too Much," *Seattle Post-Intelligencer,* September 1, 2001.
4. Benedict XVI, *Caritas in veritate,* chap. 4.

CHAPTER 8

1. Samuel Huntington, *Who Are We?* (New York: Simon & Schuster, 2004), 180.
2. John Paul II, *Message for the World Day for Migrants and Refugees,* 1987, 3.
3. John Paul II, *Message for the World Day for Migrants and· Refugees,* 1999, 6.

CHAPTER 9

1. John XXIII, *Mater et magistra,* 1961.
2. John Paul II, *Centesimus annus* on the Hundredth Anniversary of *Rerum novarum,* 1991, 3.
3. Paul Samuelson, *Economics* (New York: McGraw-Hill, 1980), 651.
4. John Paul II, *Centisimus annus,* 2.
5. John Paul II, *Ecclesia in America,* 1999, 18.
6. Cf. Pius XI, *Quadragesimo anno,* 1931, 79.

CHAPTER 10

1. Daniel C. Dennett, *Darwin's Dangerous Idea: Evolution and the Meanings of Life* (New York: Simon & Schuster, 1995), 129–30.
2. Nietzsche, *The Gay Science* (Cambridge: Cambridge University Press, 2001), 201.
3. Richard Dawkins, *The God Delusion* (London: Bantam Press, 2006), 23–24.
4. R. J. Hollingdale, *Nietzsche: The Man and His Philosophy* (Cambridge: Cambridge University Press, 1999), 98.
5. Nietzsche, *Ecce Homo* (Mineola, N.Y.: Dover Publications, 2004), 132.

6. Benedict XVI has made the powerful counterargument that, given the failures of the old modern project, it might be better for everyone, non-believers included, to act "as if God existed" (*veluti Deus daretur*). In this suggestion, he endorses Pascal's famous wager.

7. Blaise Pascal, *Pensées* (Indianapolis, Ind.: Hackett, 2004), 55.

8. *Deus caritas est*, 1.

9. John L. Allen, Jr., "Imam Speaks of Christian-Muslim Peace," *National Catholic Reporter,* March 19, 2009.

10. Meeting with the Representatives of World Religions and Religious Leaders, September 16, 1987.

11. John Paul II, *Fides et ratio,* 1998, 95.

12. John Paul II, *Fides et ratio,* 1998, 92.

13. John Paul II, *Fides et ratio,* 1998, 81.

POSTSCRIPT

1. See Charles Taylor, *A Secular Age* (Cambridge, Mass.: Harvard University Press, 2007) and Louis Dupré, *Religion and the Rise of Modern Culture* (Notre Dame, Ind.: University of Notre Dame Press, 2008).

INDEX

99; morality and, 28; secularism
as danger to, 33, 36, 37; violence
and, 197; warfare and, 129, 130
power, 5, 6, 13, 14–15, 25–26, 36, 94
prayer, 51, 56–57
preemptive strikes, 145–47
proportionality, 136–37, 138
psyche (soul), 91, 119–20, 121,
153–54

race/racism, 67–69, 74, 105, 169–70
Rawls, John, 38
reason/rationality: as basis for Catholic social teaching, 3; biology
and, 117, 121, 122; dignity and,
111; faith and, 3, 16, 30–31, 35, 61,
197–98, 199, 201, 204–6; freedom
and, 86–87, 97; globalization
and, 194–202; law and, 202; migrants and, 175; personhood and,
91, 112; religion and, 194–202,
204; religious liberty and, 50, 61;
revelation and, 197–198, 200; scientific, 39–40; secularism as danger to, 33, 34, 35, 37, 38; truth
and, 194–202, 206; universality
of, 202, 204, 206
reconciliation, theme of, 148–50
reductionism, biological, 104–5, 108
relationships: business and, 158;
economic activity and, 182, 184,
186; freedom and, 85–86, 204,
206–11; globalization and, 184,
206–11; knowing, 95–96; manipulation of, 191; peace and, 204,
206–11; unity of humanity in, 109
religion: as ambiguous word, 199;
authority in, 200; benefits/

purpose of, 1, 37; civil, 45, 46;
culture and, 79–80, 81–82, 201;
definition of, 1–2, 43, 53, 54–55;
democracy as replacement for,
45–47; Enlightenment legacy
and, 213; fading of, 5; foundation
of, 23; freedom of, 28–30, 41–45,
57, 58, 84, 85; globalization and,
194–202; goodness in, 202–4;
government disdain for, 44; government fostering/"endorsement"
of, 49, 56, 60; government relationship with, 22–23; historical,
23–24, 43, 45, 200; law and,
79–80, 81–82; meaning of,
23–24; migrants and, 165, 166,
168, 169, 171, 175; peace and, 21,
22, 210; philosophy of life and,
1, 24–25; as private, 7; reason
and, 194–202, 204; revealed, 154,
197; secularism and, 28, 32–41,
54; truth and, 194–202; violence
and, 21–22, 142, 198–99, 202,
206
religious associations/organizations,
23, 29–30, 31, 50, 54–55, 58,
59–60, 61, 82–83, 155
religious liberty, 41–45, 48–61, 203
respect, 37, 52, 54, 88, 101, 107, 147,
161, 175–76, 214
responsibility to protect, 37, 130, 132,
133, 136, 139, 142, 146, 147
revelation, 3, 7, 122, 197–98, 200,
203, 204
Revelation to John, 213–14
revenge, 134–35, 139, 148
rights: Benedict XVI UN address
about, 209; democracy and,
26–27, 42, 43; dignity and, 69;

terrorism, 131, 142–44, 145, 146, 147, 167

Tocqueville, Alexis de, 26, 83

totalitarianism, 35–36, 88, 109, 110, 197, 201

trade/commerce: barriers to, 179–80; economic activity and, 179–80, 182–83, 186–87, 190, 191–92; free, 179–80, 181, 186–87, 190, 191–92; international trade agreements and, 187, 191

transcendence, 109–10, 121, 205, 213

truth: acceptance of God's, 110; democratic institutions as danger to, 43; foundation of religion and, 23; freedom and, 27, 85–102; globalization and, 115, 194–202; God as, 85, 196; knowing and, 95–97; law and culture and, 62, 64, 65, 84, 99; morality and, 35–36, 62, 64, 65, 97, 122, 195; Nietzsche search for universal, 196; painful, 93–94, 96; a priori, 196; reason and, 194–202; religion and, 23, 24, 194–202; religious liberty and, 43, 49, 50, 51–53, 54, 60, 61; revelation and, 200, 203, 211; secularism and, 27, 34, 35–36; as universal, 196, 204, 206

unified field theory, 12–13

United Nations (UN), 63, 103, 104–6, 107, 108, 109, 114, 130, 133–34, 144, 162, 208–09

Universal Declaration on the Human Genome and Human Rights (UN), 104–6, 108, 109

Universal Declaration of the Rights of Man (UN), 114

universalism, 206, 207, 209

universe: black holes in, 113–14; chance as ruling, 11–12; creation of, 6

universities, 40, 117, 124

U.S. Conference of Catholic Bishops, 132, 136, 137, 141, 144, 145, 146, 165–66, 173, 174

utopias, 46, 88, 89, 198, 212–13

values, 5, 36, 64, 84, 115, 117, 134, 175

Vatican Council: First, 199; Second, 2–3, 48–53, 55, 57, 59–60, 65, 99, 126, 178, 187, 202–3, 209–10

Vietnam War, 131, 136

violence, 21–22, 140–41, 197–99, 201, 202, 206, 209–10

warfare: cause of, 133, 135; combatants and noncombatants in, 131, 132, 137; conducting, 130, 136–41; and decision to go to war, 133, 134, 135, 144; forgiveness and, 127–28, 139, 147–50; globalization and, 133–34, 135; intent and purpose of, 129, 134–36; justifiable, 128–29; as last resort, 135; national sovereignty and, 133–34; peace and, 126–28, 134–36, 139, 147, 148–49; public opinion and, 137–38; self-defense and, 129, 130, 134, 143, 147; weapons in, 131–32, 136, 137, 138, 144–45, 146

Washington, George: Farewell Address of, 36–37